DELICATESSEN

DELICATESSEN

A Celebration and Cookbook

Rosemary Moon

DAVID & CHARLES
Newton Abbot London

This book is for Ear'ole, who has been as enthusiastic about my shop as she has been about all the other things that I have tackled, and then begged her to help with.

With very special thanks to:

John Plimmer and all the staff at RPM Photographic, Havant, Hants. To John, for taking the snaps, and to all the others for keeping us going with cups of tea.

William Morris of Arundel, for the loan of the fine china and crystal for the photographs.

My husband Nick, for his enthusiasm and endless help.

British Library Cataloguing in Publication Data
Moon, Rosemary
    Delicatessen.
    1. Food
    I. Title
    641.3

ISBN 0 7153 9315 4

Typeset by Typesetters (Birmingham) Ltd
Smethwick   Warley   West Midlands
and printed in Portugal by Resopal
for David & Charles Publishers plc
Brunel House   Newton Abbot   Devon

Colour origination by Columbia Offset

CONTENTS

INTRODUCTION

Travel has undoubtedly broadened our culinary horizons and ingredients that were only ever found in markets on holidays abroad are now readily available in specialist shops and large supermarkets. It is wonderful to have this array of foods accessible to us, but it is even more exciting when you know a little about the food, how it is produced, how to prepare it and how it should be served.

A good delicatessen or deli counter in a large supermarket should be run by enthusiastic, trained staff who will be willing to share their knowledge and love of food with you. Chatting often produces some very interesting ideas for serving and preparing the food and all of us can learn something from each other in casual conversation.

Many delicatessen foods should be eaten and appreciated just as they are, requiring no elaborate preparation or cooking. If you are paying a little more for the food you should enjoy it for what it is - avoid recipes which suggest such things as stuffing breasts of chicken with Parma ham mousse, then wrapping them in smoked salmon and poaching in wine before serving with a cream sauce. The money spent could pay for a whole dinner party.

Delicatessen: A Celebration and Cookbook will delight the enthusiastic cook who is interested in making the most of the very best ingredients. I cannot promise to make you into a world authority on ingredients, but I do hope to share my passion for good food with you, and to inspire you to try a different type of tea or a new way of serving pasta. I have kept to foods which I hope you will be able to find locally - there is no point in inspiring you with mouthwatering descriptions of cheeses available only in small mountain villages in the Alps!

A good retailer will enthuse about his stock and tempt you to try new foods. Take advantage of this knowledge and enjoy trying all that is offered to you in your delicatessen
it really is an endless delight.

COLD MEATS
& CHARCUTERIE

COLD MEATS
& CHARCUTERIE

Why is it that so often we think of pork as suitable only for roasting, for chops or sausages? Remembering bacon and ham, the versatility of the pig can be stretched to pies, sandwiches and ham, egg and chips. Yet a walk into any delicatessen or a continental charcuterie will prove the enormous potential of this vastly under-rated animal.

Pork was the staple diet of most Europeans for many centuries and it was said that the peasants of Britain lived on bread, bacon and beer. The pigs took care of themselves, scavenging and digging for food and eating virtually anything that they found in the streets of villages and towns alike. For a peasant farmer, the pig was a good investment, being almost totally edible after it had provided very rich fertiliser during its lifetime.

Pork is still eaten throughout the world and in the Far East it is a very important ingredient in many stir-fried dishes as it is tender and cooks quickly. In the UK, there has been a revival in the traditional art of sausage-making and strict regulations now dictate the maximum quantity of cereal filler allowed in the not-so-humble British banger. The addition of herbs and spices in many combinations produces a wonderful variety of flavoursome sausages to grace any supper table, but it is really only black pudding, a breakfast sausage made with large pieces of pork back fat and pig's blood, thickened with a cereal (usually oatmeal or barley), that survives as a similar food to the continental salami or saucissons.

(*page* 9) 1 French ham sausage; 2 German pepper salame; 3 Italian Milano salame; 4 French garlic sausage; 5 French pistachio sausage with beef; 6 German Cervelat

SALAMI & SAUCISSONS

It has been said that it is best not to know too much about salami and other sausages, in the same way that ignorance about haggis aids its enjoyment and easy digestion. Sausage-making is recorded in histories of the Roman Empire and the words sausage, salami and saucissons are all derived from the Latin *salsus*, meaning 'salted'. These days the word salame is also used to refer to an idiot with less brains than a sack of potatoes!

All salami are raw meat, usually pork but sometimes with the addition of a little beef. The flavour of each sausage is mainly determined by the proportion of meat to fat, the meatier sausage usually being the sweetest. The most usual flavouring additions are spices, peppercorns and nuts, especially pistachios. Some salami are wrapped in garlic or herbs which give additional flavour. The white dust often found on the casing of salami is bacterial and usually contributes to the flavour of the sausage. Garlic is seldom put into salami as it would mould and cause the sausage to deteriorate, so the garlic-like flavour is achieved by a combination of other flavouring ingredients.

All products grouped collectively under the name charcuterie must be treated in some way to ensure the products' keeping qualities. The most common methods are smoking, drying or curing, or a combination of two of these processes may be used.

Salami are usually air-dried at a constant temperature during which time they lose well over a quarter and up to a third of their original weight through evaporation of the water content. The size of the sausage will determine how long the drying process will take, but it is of paramount importance that the meat is perfectly dry if it is to store well.

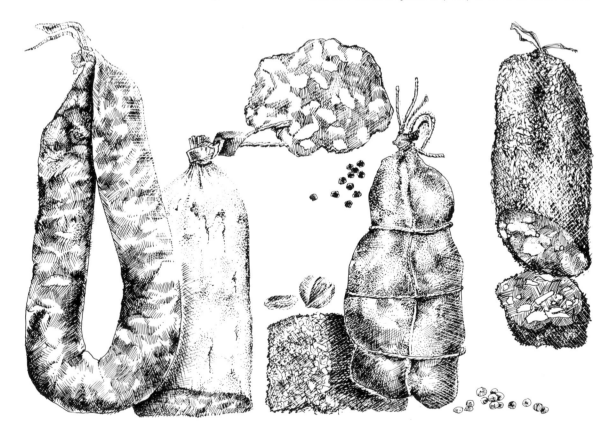

(l to r) York ham on the bone; home cooked honey-roast ham; pâté de campagne; haslet; smoked turkey; raw Bradenham ham (hanging in background)

Milano is the variety that I regard as the standard among the enormous range of Italian salami. It is minced fairly finely with a high proportion of fat to meat and has a good spicy flavour which is not too hot, although peppercorns and other spices are often included. Napoli is also a very popular variety, having coarser lumps of fat than the Milano and being made with a mixture of pork and beef. I find that Napoli is slightly chewy but delicious. Italian salami often contain a mixture of pork and beef, whereas the French are more likely to keep to a pure pork sausage. Small metal tags on the string coatings of Italian salami will indicate the meat content - those stamped 'S' are made with pork only, whereas mixtures of pork and beef are marked 'SB'. I also try to have one very hot salame always in stock - Ventracini and Murghetto are the usual choice. These are both very peppery, but the full effect is often not realised until you swallow.

Although it is most usual to think of salami as an Italian speciality, they are, in fact, made throughout Europe. The most popular German salami that I sell is the square peppery variety, which is very finely minced pork and beef coated on the outside with ground black peppercorns (see p7). German salami are often quite heavily smoked. Hungarian salami, a small sausage approx 5cm/2in in diameter, is very hard and spicy and is an excellent ingredient in quiches and pizzas. The meat used for Danish salami is pre-salted (saltpetre is included) which explains its very vivid pink colouring and its salty flavour. I always feel that Danish salami lack the finesse of many other varieties and their inferior quality is reflected in the price, which is generally considerably lower. The most widely sold of the French salami in the UK are the plump, sweet Jesus de Lyon and the Arles, from the gastronomically famed region of that name.

It is impossible to describe any but the most popular of the salami that are found both in delicatessens and supermarkets. It is quite acceptable to ask to sample before you buy, although this is only possible if you are purchasing over the counter. Always ask for a slice cut freshly from the salame and do not expect to get the true flavour from a pre-cut chunk on a plate.

HINTS FOR BUYING SALAME

Uncut salami keep perfectly at a cool room temperature and may often be found festooning a delicatessen's ceiling. Once cut, however, they should be treated as any other cold meat and kept under refrigeration, usually with the cut end covered - do not buy from a cut salame which is not refrigerated. A good delicatessen will always remove the casing from a salame before slicing it, unless it is wrapped in garlic or herbs, but only enough should be removed for the immediate customer. Resist being served from a salame where all the casing has already been removed - the meat may have become dry and tough during storage. If you wish to purchase a chunk of salame to slice yourself in the future, you should ask for the casing to be left on the meat to keep it in prime condition. It is usual for all salami to be sliced very finely.

COOKING WITH SALAMI

Apart from using the ends of the sausages in sauces, it is generally best not to cook with these meats but just to enjoy them cold. Salami are best served as an antipasto, in sandwiches, with salads or eaten with a little cheese and fresh crusty bread. There was a time when a popular cocktail food was salame (usually Danish) rolled round a cream or cottage cheese filling to form a cornet. Luckily, this fashion seems to have passed as such things were never very easy to eat in a dignified way.

Should you arrive at a delicatessen counter when a salame is just being started or finished, you may be lucky enough to collect the end chunk which can be used to give extra flavour to spaghetti sauces or risotto-type dishes. I find that the finer, harder salami are best for adding to recipes, but remember that they contain a high proportion of fat, so adjust oil or butter in the recipe accordingly.

SUPPERTIME RISOTTO
Serves 2–3

This simple risotto provides a filling supper dish and may be made with an end chunk of salame. Left-over cold meat from a joint may also be added together with any vegetables that are to hand when you add the salame.

2 × 15ml/tbsp olive oil
1 onion, finely sliced
1 clove garlic, crushed
225g/8oz/1 cup risotto rice, thoroughly washed in running water
1 × 5ml/tsp powdered saffron (optional)

186g/6½oz can pimentos, drained and chopped
175g/6oz salame, finely chopped
500ml/1pt/2½ cups boiling water or vegetable stock
2×15ml/tbsp freshly chopped parsley
salt and freshly ground black pepper
25-50g/1-2oz Parmesan cheese, freshly grated

1 · Heat the oil in a large pan over a moderate heat, add the onion and garlic and cook, covered, until well softened and just starting to brown.
2 · Add the rice and saffron and sauté for a few minutes with the onion until opaque.
3 · Add the pimentos, salame and boiling water or stock to the pan with most, but not all, of the parsley and a little salt and pepper. Return to the boil, stirring once or twice.
4 · Simmer, covered, for about 20min until all the liquid has been absorbed.
5 · Remove from the heat and season to taste with salt and pepper, then stir in the Parmesan cheese. Leave for a minute or so, until the cheese has melted, then serve, sprinkled with the remaining parsley.

COOK'S NOTE: *Risotto rice is generally served slightly wet (see Rice, p57) and is usually in a fairly rib-sticking form! Slivers of butter are often added just before serving (see Risotto Milanese, p58), but I like to add Parmesan to this recipe for extra flavour, especially if the salame is the only meat being used.*

SMOKED, SCALDED, DRIED OR COOKED
–YET MORE SAUSAGES

Many varieties of sausages are not classed as salami at all, these coming mainly from Germany, Poland and other mid-European countries. They are usually smoked or scalded to preserve the meat, but some, such as haslet and liver sausage, are totally cooked. It is simplest to describe them according to how they have been preserved.

Smoked Dried Sausages
Without doubt the best known and most readily available variety in the UK is Cervelat from Germany (see p7). It is a finely ground mixture of pork and beef with a comparatively bland seasoning. The sausage is smoked until it is golden-brown. The wide availability of Cervelat in supermarkets and delicatessens makes it one of the most popular of charcuterie products and one that will not offend even the most conservative of palates.

Teewurst is another German example of this type of sausage and is usually sold in small packs. It is a smooth spreading sausage, similar in texture to a fine liver sausage, with a bright pink colour. Teewurst has a rich and pronounced smoked flavour and is delicious on hot toast or crackers.

The best examples are made from pure pork, but cheaper varieties may also contain some beef.

Mettwurst is similar to Teewurst but is always made from a mixture of pork and beef, is very smoky and often contains paprika to give it a more spicy flavour. It is available smooth for spreading, or of a coarser texture for slicing when it may be heated before serving.

Extrawurst or Fleischwurst is another lightly smoked sausage for eating cold but may also be poached or grilled. These sausages sometimes contain nuts or garlic which give extra texture to an otherwise smooth paste.

Scalded or Lightly Cooked Sausages

These are generally large sausages that are sold for slicing, mainly to be eaten cold, but some are good for cooking. The scalding or light cooking of these products acts to preserve them. Bierwurst is a large German sausage that may be pork or pork and beef, has a fine texture and is usually spiced with peppercorns and white mustard seed. There is no beer in the sausage, but it is a traditional accompaniment to the brew. Bierschinkenwurst is a coarser textured Bierwurst incorporating small pieces of ham. Frankfurters are the most widely known of all the scalded sausages, and many other varieties such as Bockwurst, Knackwurst and Weinerwurst are really the same thing but in different sizes. To my taste, none of these have a particularly distinctive flavour, but the quality in texture is immediately obvious. The best of these sausages are loose or in jars - I find that the necessary temperatures achieved during canning tend to make the sausages rather fatty and slimy in texture.

Garlic sausages are made in many countries, notably France, Germany and Poland. I sell most of the French variety, which is a small sausage with a strong flavour but a coarse and fatty texture. German garlic sausages tend to be milder, while the Polish varieties are hard in texture and small in size. Mortadella is the most popular Italian example of the scalded sausages; it is usually very large and always contains chunks of fat in the smooth meat paste. The best Mortadella also includes pistachio nuts, the texture and flavour of which relieve an otherwise bland but pleasant meat.

Within this category of sausages are several harder and spicier varieties which are excellent when added to cassoulet-type dishes or bean stews. These are, namely, chorizos and kabanos. Chorizos are always peppery, flavoured with paprika and although they sound Spanish, are often made in Germany. They are generally quite small, about 225/8oz in weight, but some of the German varieties are large and intended to be sold sliced. They usually need to be cooked and I use them a great deal with beans and in Mexican dishes, slicing them before cooking. Kabanos are much thinner than chorizos but are used in much the same way, although the older, drier varieties are popular as chewing sausages. Many of the branded 'pepper salame sticks' sold in supermarkets are variations on the theme of the kabanos, sold very fresh before they harden.

The Polish sausages Wieska and Tuchowska are generally sold in rings for slicing and heating, although they may also be eaten cold. Wieska is my favourite of the two, being leaner and drier.

Cooked or Boiled Sausages

Many of the meats in this category may not immediately be labelled as sausages in your mind, but this is where they fit in the standard delicatessen classification. They are usually made from pig's offal or blood.

Black pudding is the most common of these sausages in the UK. It is made from blood thickened with cereals and contains large pieces of fat. You either love it or hate it. It is usually sliced, fried and eaten for breakfast. If you really want to experiment, try it with bacon, tomatoes and fried bananas. The Germans, French and Poles all make variations on this traditional dish. Brawn is usually square in shape and therefore quite unlike a sausage, although it is classified as one. I have never eaten brawn - no doubt I should - so cannot comment on it except to say that it is made from the pig's head which is simmered with herbs and spices; the resulting meat is set in the naturally produced aspic. It has always had about the same amount of appeal to me as sheep's eyes. As a confirmed haggis lover, that just proves how irrational we humans can be!

Haslet is a pork meat loaf, which is flavoured with a variety of herbs and spices. With the addition of plenty of hot English mustard, it makes one of my favourite sandwiches. It is peculiarly English and should be bought from a round loaf, covered in strings of fat which give it flavour. Loaf-tin shaped varieties are seldom tasty or worth eating and are often cooked without the flavoursome larding of fat.

Haggis is the famed dish of Scotland. It is made from the liver, lungs and heart of a sheep with the addition of oatmeal and spices, all of which is packed into the sheep's stomach. Natural stomachs are not often used now and the casing should be well pricked before the haggis is simmered in a pan of water for 30-40 min. Haggis also reheats well in the microwave cooker; approximately 10min should be allowed for a 450g/1lb example on a setting of 70% power. Haggis is traditionally washed down with whisky. I have also sliced a haggis and cooked it as burgers over the barbecue on a piece of foil - it makes a change from beefburgers.

Liver sausage may be firm for slicing or smooth for spreading and most of the continental varieties are of the latter type. The sausage is generally made from pork liver and the price paid dictates the quality received. Very expensive liver sausages may be made from calves' or goose livers, but these are difficult to find and very rich in taste.

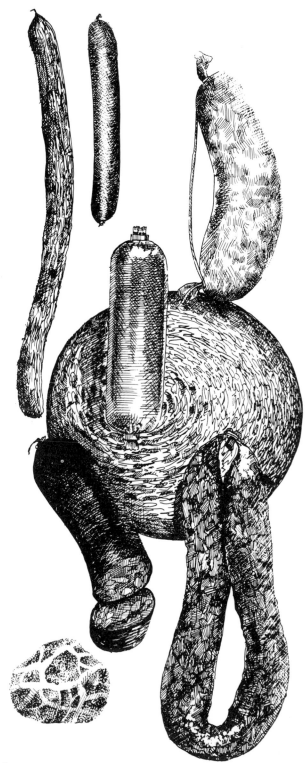

HINTS FOR BUYING PRESERVED SAUSAGES

All these products should be kept under refrigeration unless, like some members of the Frankfurter family, they are preserved in a jar or can. Slicing sausages should be stored in a chiller with the cut end always covered. Don't worry if the first slice is slightly discoloured - the meat is simply oxidising. The retailer should not sell you the first slice and the second cut should be of a bright, usually pink colour. If the sausage is discoloured all the way through, do not buy it. Keep any sliced meat in the refrigerator until it is required.

HAMS

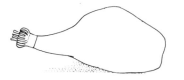

There is a world of difference between ham that has been sliced from the bone or cut from a joint on a machine and the pre-packaged wet and tasteless substance that so many people believe to be ham. We always have a boiled ham on the bone in our delicatessen counter and it is without doubt the single main item responsible for drawing people into the shop who might otherwise be content to look through the window.

A true ham is the whole rear leg of the pig and is cut from the carcase before it is prepared. If the leg is cured while it is still attached, it is technically a gammon - hence the confusion caused by the term 'gammon ham'.

PARMA HAM

Parma is perhaps the most famous of all the dried hams and is air-dried in a similar way to many salami. Being an air-dried product, Parma ham is raw and should be referred to as 'prosciutto crudo' - *prosciutto* is the Italian word for ham and may refer to cheaper hams that may look like Parma but are not. True prosciutto crudo has the brand name stamped into its skin and is always from the Parma area of Italy.

Parma hams are rubbed with a mixture of sea salt and other spices and the process is repeated twice before the hams are left to dry. According to size this may take between eight and twenty-four months. At the end of the drying process, the hams are rubbed with very fine pepper and this may be clearly seen on the back of the meat where it is not covered with the thick brown skin.

Tips for Buying Parma Ham

First, even if you are in Italy, expect to pay a high price for Parma ham - anything that seems a real bargain will probably not be true prosciutto crudo. Only buy a whole ham if you are really going to use it. You can freeze it, but it will start to go rancid after a comparatively short storage period of three months. You will also need to consider slicing. It is not fair to expect your local delicatessen to do it for you as it takes a long time to slice the whole ham and Parma must be cut thinly. If you attempt to cut it with a knife, remove the thick brown skin from the portion to be sliced, paying great attention to the direction in which you are cutting - it is very easy for the knife to slip and the blade must travel away from you. Only cut the amount required at one time, otherwise the extra slices will dry out during storage. The ham is always easier to cut when it is well chilled and may be even easier to handle if it is lightly frozen.

Parma ham is available ready sliced in small packets, but this is an expensive way to buy it, although it does always ensure good, even pieces.

Cooking with Parma Ham

Most people think of serving this delicacy with slices of ripe melon as a starter, but it also makes an excellent accompaniment to many of the exotic fruits that are widely available in greengrocers and supermarkets. I particularly enjoy Parma ham with slices of ripe mango (see p19) or paw-paw (also called papaya), and it is also delicious with fresh figs.

Although the idea of cooking with Parma ham sounds prohibitively expensive, it need not be so. The Smoked Trout & Parma Ham Mousse (see p18) is merely decorated with slices of the ham and the Carbonnade of Beef is enriched by using diced ham instead of bacon. Ask your local delicatessen to keep the end of a new Parma ham for you, or put in a bid for the unsliceable knuckle end. Such pieces are also excellent for adding to spaghetti sauces and for mincing with other meats for meatballs, again to serve with pasta.

OTHER CONTINENTAL HAMS

Although regional hams are produced throughout Europe, few are particularly well known. Of these, the French Bayonne and the German Westphalian hams are the most popular and the easiest to obtain.

The Bayonne is a raw ham cured at Orthez in south-west France. Its particular flavour is achieved by the addition of red wine and rosemary to the brine in which it is cured. The ham is then lightly smoked. It is very similar in appearance to Parma ham. Westphalian ham is darker in colour than Parma ham and Bayonne; it is more heavily smoked than Bayonne and is aged before selling.

CARBONNADE OF BEEF
Serves 6-8 (see p19)

This very rich and delicious dish should be served with plain boiled rice or jacket potatoes and a boiled or steamed green vegetable such as Calabrese or Brussels sprouts. The casserole is topped with a thick-set natural yoghurt which offsets the richness of the meat.

2 × 15ml/tbsp olive oil
225g/8oz Parma ham, cut into very small dice
1 large onion, thinly sliced
775g/1¾lb braising steak, cut into large dice
2 × 15ml/tbsp flour
375ml/15fl oz/2 cups brown ale or stout
2 bay leaves
1 × 15ml/tbsp Dijon mustard
salt and freshly ground black pepper
set natural or Greek yogurt for serving
chopped chives to garnish

1 · Pre-heat the oven to gas mark 3/160°C/325°F.
2 · Heat the olive oil in a large casserole or pan, add the Parma ham and the onion, cover and cook over a low heat for 10min, stirring once or twice.
3 · Add the braising steak to the pan and brown on all sides over a higher heat. Remove the meat and onions from the pan using a slotted spoon.
4 · Stir the flour into the remaining juices and cook slowly until well browned, stirring all the time. This may take several minutes, but do not be impatient otherwise the sauce will be pale and uninteresting instead of a rich dark brown colour.
5 · Remove the pan from the heat and gradually add the beer, stirring constantly. Bring the sauce to the boil.
6 · Return the meats and onions to the pan and add the bay leaves, mustard and salt and pepper. If the pan is not suitable for use in the oven, transfer the meat to a casserole dish. Cover and cook in the pre-heated oven for 2½-3hr, until the beef is tender.
7 · Remove the bay leaves and season the casserole to taste. Serve topped with yogurt and garnished with freshly chopped chives.

COOK'S TIP: *Always break the bay leaves before adding them to the pan otherwise most of their flavour will be trapped and they will be of no benefit to the casserole.*

SMOKED TROUT & PARMA HAM MOUSSE
Serves 8 (see p19)

The flavours of the trout and ham combine beautifully in this starter, which can be served either with melon balls mounted in the centre or set into the mixture. The recipe is also delicious if it is made with smoked salmon pieces, but the trout is a little more unusual. Use smoked rainbow trout – salmon trout is an unnecessary extravagance.

250ml/8fl oz/1 cup milk
6 peppercorns
1 blade mace
small piece celery
small piece carrot
small piece onion
25g/1oz butter
25g/1oz flour
salt and white pepper to taste
175g/6oz Parma ham slices
450g/1lb smoked trout, flaked
250ml/10fl oz/1¼ cups double or thick cream
3×15ml/tbsp boiling water
1×heaped 15ml/tbsp gelatine (1 sachet)
2 egg whites
1 ripe melon, balled
toast fingers or Melba toasts to serve

1 · Heat the milk with the peppercorns, mace and vegetables until almost boiling, then remove from the heat, cover and leave for 10min. This may be done by heating in a jug in the microwave for 4min, then cover the jug and leave for 10min.

2 · Prepare a bechamel sauce with the flavoured milk. Melt the butter, add the flour and cook for a few seconds, then gradually add the milk, straining it into the roux mixture. Beat thoroughly while adding the milk, then return the sauce to the heat and bring to the boil, stirring constantly. Season to taste with salt and white pepper, then cover the sauce with greaseproof paper to prevent it from forming a skin and allow it to cool completely. (The sauce may also be prepared in a microwave cooker.)

3 · Prepare a 23-25cm/9-10in ring mould. Lightly oil a plastic mould and line with greaseproof paper or baking parchment. Metal moulds should also be lightly oiled. Lay the slices of Parma ham in the mould to make a covering for the mousse; slightly overlap the slices of ham.

4 · Place the cooled sauce and the trout in a liquidiser or food processor and blend until smooth. Whip the cream until thick but still soft. Fold the trout mixture into the cream.

5 · Sprinkle the gelatine onto the boiling water in a small bowl and stir well - then leave for a minute or so to dissolve. If the powder is not completely dissolved, place the bowl in a saucepan of water and heat gently or heat in the microwave for 20sec - do not let the gelatine boil.

6 · Allow the gelatine to cool, then add to the trout cream.

7 · Whisk the egg whites until stiff, then add to the cream. Place a layer of the mixture in the base of the prepared mould, then arrange the melon balls on top, if they are to be set into the mousse. Carefully spoon the remaining trout mixture into the mould.

8 · Fold the ends of the Parma ham slices over the filling, then refrigerate for 2-3hr until set.

9 · To serve, ease the mousse away from the edges of the mould, then invert it onto a serving plate and shake firmly to release the mousse. Pile the melon balls into the centre of the mousse if they have not been set into the mixture.

10 · Serve with freshly cooked toast fingers or Melba toasts.

COOK'S NOTE: *Commercially prepared Melba toasts are available, but they are nothing like the real thing. Use pre-sliced white bread and remove the crusts. Toast on both sides under a grill, then carefully slice through horizontally, using a sharp thin-bladed bread saw. Toast the newly cut surfaces but keep a watchful eye on them as the toast is now very thin and will cook extra quickly.*

(front to back) Parma Ham with Fresh Mango; Smoked Trout & Parma Ham Mousse; Carbonnade of Beef

THE TRADITIONAL HAMS OF BRITAIN AND THE USA

Many of the most famous hams are British, which makes it all the more shameful that many shops are selling the wet and tasteless erzatz ham that we are all familiar with. York ham is renowned throughout the world, although other hams are less well known. All the hams are dry salted to preserve the meat by extracting the juices which would otherwise cause the meat to perish. While the period of maturing is seldom described as such, the hams are thoroughly air-dried after being treated with a mixture of sugars and spices; they are also often smoked before drying. Oak is the most commonly used wood for smoking meat in the UK but other varieties are also used and all contribute to the final flavour of the ham. After drying, the following hams are soaked in water to remove any excessive saltiness from the curing and then cooked, unlike the continental hams described earlier. A dried, uncooked ham will keep for several months in dry cool conditions.

CARVING A HAM ON THE BONE
Should you ever possess a whole ham on the bone, you must know how to carve it properly, otherwise you will waste a great deal of meat and subsequently be eating ham soup for ages.

Securing the ham (so that it doesn't run away from you) will be the first problem. If you have a ham stand, all well and good, otherwise invert a large plate and stand the ham on that; it will raise the meat sufficiently to allow your carving knife to travel as required during slicing.

You will need to turn the ham over twice during carving to remove the maximum amount of meat. I always start at the fillet end and work towards the knuckle. Always aim to be carving at right angles to the bone, otherwise the sliced meat will be stringy in appearance and texture.

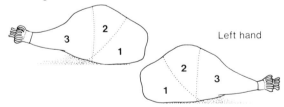

Right hand

Left hand

1 · Start from the fillet or thick end of the ham. Remove the first slice, then continue carving until approximately one third of the way down the ham. Cut down to the bone to avoid excessive wastage.
2 · Turn the ham over and continue slicing the middle third of the ham.
3 · Turn the ham over again and finish carving the ham to the knuckle end.

HAM & LENTIL SOUP
Serves 6
Many delicatessens will sell their ham bones but you should be prepared to put your name on a waiting list. After trimming most of the meat away, the bones will make marvellous stock or soup. Ensure that any resulting stock is not too salty before you add it to casseroles or other recipes.

125g/4oz/¾ cup red lentils
1 large onion, sliced
1 large carrot, diced
2 sticks celery, finely sliced
125g/4oz ham, from the bone, cut into small pieces
1 litre/2pt/4½ cups ham stock
2 bay leaves
freshly ground black pepper
salt to taste

1 · Rinse the lentils in a sieve under running water, then place them in a large saucepan with all the remaining ingredients except the salt.
2 · Bring the soup to the boil, stirring from time to time, then simmer slowly for 45-60min, until the vegetables are soft and the lentils have cooked and thickened the soup.
3 · Remove the bay leaves. Season the soup to taste with salt and pepper and serve with fresh crusty bread.

COOK'S NOTE: *Red lentils do not require soaking (see p38). If you have not made stock from the bone, place the whole bone or part of it in the pan with the measured amount of water, not stock. The bone will give plenty of flavour to the soup during cooking and should be removed before the soup is seasoned prior to serving.*

YORK HAM (see p10)

Perhaps the most famous of all, this ham is dry cured when it is rubbed with salt and then matured for 3-4 months. It is simmered slowly after it has been soaked and is usually coated with breadcrumbs before it is sold. York ham commands a high price and is much sought after, especially at Christmas time. It will be interesting to see whether, in the future, the generation that is now being raised on comparatively low salt diets will consider the York ham to be as special as those who now remember it so fondly.

BRADENHAM HAMS (see p11)

In its uncooked form, the Bradenham ham is easily distinguishable by its very dark, almost black appearance and the brand mark Bradenham stamped into its skin. These hams are from Chippenham in Wiltshire, where they have been prepared since 1781. They are rubbed with salt to dry cure them and then coated with a mixture of spices, including juniper, and molasses, which is mainly responsible for the black appearance of the ham. After curing, the hams are soaked and then simmered, black treacle usually being added to the water in which they are cooked. As with all hams, the thick skin is removed before sale or serving. Bradenham hams should be presented uncrumbed or coated in white breadcrumbs.

SUFFOLK HAM

Lesser known than the Bradenham, the Suffolk is also a sweet ham which is lightly smoked.

It must also be said that a plain boiled ham presented on or off the bone is a delight to the jaded palate and should not be ignored because it remains undistinguished by any special cure. When bought in large pieces, such hams may be further enhanced by baking for a short time in a hot oven with a glaze of either honey, ginger syrup, marmalade mixed with orange juice or fruit syrups.

VIRGINIA & SMITHFIELD
The Hams of the USA

These hams are dry cured in the same way as many of the English hams, but their distinctive flavours were traditionally achieved by feeding the pigs on special foods. Virginia hams were taken from pigs that were fed on peanuts and peaches while those producing Smithfield hams enjoyed a diet of acorns and other nuts. I wonder whether these diets are still adhered to?

OTHER DELICATESSEN MEATS

It is quite usual to find large joints of roast beef and pork for slicing on the delicatessen counter, but two of the more interesting meats to reach us in recent years have been smoked turkey and pastrami.

Smoked turkey (see p11) is produced in many countries, but my preference is for the Belgian variety. Available on or off the bone, the meat is usually from only the breasts of the birds and is lightly smoked, moist and quite delicious. Smoked turkey may be sliced thickly and eaten hot or served cold, with or in salads (see p27). Smoked chicken is also popular and smoked pheasant makes a treat.

Pastrami, made famous outside the United States by the television series *Kojak*, in which the hero ate this meat on rye bread, is salted and spiced brisket of beef. I prefer it coated in very coarsely grated black pepper and it should always be sliced extremely thinly. Pastrami cut from a very regular block will probably not be made from brisket of beef, so the odder the shape, the better the meat. Bresaola is a similar dried salt beef from Italy, but is often not quite as lean as pastrami.

Corned beef is a traditional favourite and should not be totally forgotten in favour of other more refined (and more expensive) meats. Corning was originally a process of preservation achieved by rubbing the meat with corns or grains of salt. The corned beef that we are familiar with is a cured beef which is then boiled and pressed before being canned. Mainly produced in South America, a good quality corned beef is delicious served cold with pickles or hot with potatoes in a hash.

A Tavola!

There is a great deal more to Italian food than an endless variety of pasta shapes topped with Bolognese sauce, and pizzas. Italy is famed for its salami, sausages and Parma hams (see pp8-18), its cheeses and olive oils, but there is still much about the cuisine that is relatively unknown. What could you include with mixed salami to make a really interesting dish of antipasto? I suggest Marinated Aubergines and Cannellini Bean & Tuna Fish Salad for a good combination of colours and textures.

Homemade pizzas often lack even a vague hint of authenticity. The secret is the dough for the base and the use of Mozzarella for the topping. There are some excellent commercial pesto sauces available, but always be prepared to pay for one made with olive oil and not a lighter, less flavoursome oil. If you are following the recipe opposite for Pesto alla Genovese, do try to get some Pecorino to mix with the Parmesan – it is a sharp ewes' milk cheese that really adds an extra bite to any pasta dish.

(*l to r*) Torta Dolcelatte; Parmesan; Penne pasta; Gorgonzola; Tortellini pasta; Mozzarella; Grissini breadsticks; Mortadella; Milano salame (*above*); Ventricini salame (*below*); Pasta with Pesto alla Genovese

Smoked Quails' Eggs & Mozzarella Salad

Italian specialities can easily be combined with foods from other countries. Mozzarella cheese adds flavour and an unusual texture to any salad - combine it with smoked quails' eggs for a very special starter. The salad may be served on a bed of raw spinach. Serves 4 (see p27)

2 ripe avocados, peeled and sliced
lemon juice
2×200g/7oz Mozzarella cheese, sliced
4 large flavoursome tomatoes, sliced
1×15ml/tbsp freshly chopped mixed herbs
12 smoked quails' eggs
4×15ml/tbsp set natural yogurt
salt and freshly ground black pepper
4×15ml/tbsp virgin olive oil
crusty bread for serving

1 · Sprinkle the avocado slices with lemon juice, then arrange them with Mozzarella and tomato slices.
2 · Scatter the freshly chopped herbs over the tomatoes and lightly season with salt and black pepper.
3 · Place 1×15ml/tbsp natural yogurt in the centre of each plate and top with three quails' eggs.
4 · Trickle a little oil over each salad. Serve with fresh bread.

Pesto alla Genovese

This traditional sauce of basil, garlic and cheese should always be made with best quality virgin olive oil. It makes approximately 375ml/15fl oz/ 2 cups - sufficient for 8 servings as a starter.

125g/4oz/2 cups fresh basil leaves, torn
    from their stalks and chopped or
    75g/3oz/1½ cups parsley and 5×5ml/tsp
    dried basil
½×5ml/tsp salt
½×5ml/tsp freshly ground black pepper
3-4 cloves garlic, chopped
50g/2oz/⅓ cup pine kernels
250ml/10fl oz/1¼ cups virgin olive oil, approx
50g/2oz/1 cup freshly grated Parmesan and
    Pecorino cheese, mixed
pine kernels to garnish

1 · Chop all the ingredients together in a liquidiser or food processor, then gradually add sufficient olive oil to give a smooth paste.
2 · If you have no blender pound the dry ingredients in a pestle and mortar, then gradually stir in the oil.
3 · Stir the sauce into freshly cooked pasta which has been tossed in butter. Sprinkle with pine kernels and serve immediately.

Antipasto

Here are two ideas to complement your own selection of salami and sausages.

Marinated Aubergines
Serves 4-6

450g/1lb aubergines, halved lengthways
  then thickly sliced
3×15ml/tbsp white wine or garlic vinegar
1 clove garlic, crushed
1×5ml/tsp freshly chopped basil
1×5ml/tsp freshly chopped oregano
salt and freshly ground black pepper
3×15ml/tbsp virgin olive oil
1×15ml/tbsp capers (optional)

1 · Simmer the aubergines in a large pan of water until just cooked, about 10min, or cook, covered, in the microwave for 7-8min or until just tender. Drain.
2 · Mix together the vinegar, garlic, herbs, salt and pepper in a large bowl, then add the aubergine slices and toss until coated in the dressing. Leave until cold, toss, then cover and chill in the refrigerator for at least 1hr.
3 · Add the olive oil and capers just before serving and toss again.

Cannellini Bean & Tuna Fish Salad
Serves 4-6

2×400g/14oz can cannellini beans, drained
  and rinsed
3×15ml/tbsp virgin olive oil
juice of ½ lemon
1×15ml/tbsp freshly chopped spring onions
2×15ml/tbsp freshly chopped parsley
salt and freshly ground black pepper
1×200g/7oz can tuna fish

1 · Shake the cannellini beans dry, then place them in a bowl.
2 · Place the oil, lemon juice, spring onions, parsley and seasonings in a small screw top jar and shake well. Pour the dressing over the beans. Chill in the refrigerator for at least 1hr.
3 · Flake the tuna fish; dispose of any brine, but if the fish is packed in olive oil it may be added to the dressing for the beans.
4 · Serve the salad on a plate with the flaked tuna arranged on top of the beans.

COOK'S NOTE: I have also prepared this dish using flageolet beans. This is not so authentic but the green beans give an attractive appearance to the dish.

Pizza
Serves 2-4 (see p110)

Pizza is one of the most popular Italian dishes to be exported around the world, after the many variations on pasta. Pizza dough is more oily than a standard bread dough. It should be rolled thinly and cooked very quickly. Adding sun-dried tomatoes as a garnish to the pizza gives a strong savoury taste.

450g/1lb/4 cups strong white bread flour
1×5ml/tsp salt
125ml/5fl oz/²/₃ cups olive oil or pizza oil
25g/1oz fresh yeast
pinch caster sugar
250ml/10oz/1¼ cups, approx, warm water
350ml/15fl oz/2 cups prepared tomato sauce for pasta
125g/4oz sliced pizza sausage, sardines, salame, etc,
  if required
8 sun-dried tomato halves, chopped
450g/1lb Mozzarella cheese, grated or finely sliced
4×15ml/tbsp grated Parmesan cheese
8×15ml/tbsp olive oil

1 · Place the flour in a large bowl with the salt and oil. Cream the yeast with the sugar and a little of the warm water. Add to the flour and mix to a manageable dough, adding more water as required. Knead thoroughly on a lightly floured surface until the dough is smooth and elastic.
2 · Place the dough in a clean bowl and cover with cling film. Leave in a warm place for 1-1½hr, until well risen and doubled in size.
3 · Pre-heat the oven to gas mark 8/250°C/450°F.
4 · Turn the dough out onto a lightly floured surface and knead gently. Divide into four and make each piece of dough into a circle approx 25cm/10in in diameter. Use a combination of rolling with a pin and pressing with the heel of your hand to make the circle. Place the dough on greased baking sheets, raising the edges of each piece slightly to contain the topping.
5 · Spoon the pizza sauce onto the dough and top with the ingredient of your choice, or leave plain for a tomato pizza.
6 · Scatter the Mozzarella over the pizzas, then garnish with the chopped sun-dried tomatoes. Top each pizza with grated Parmesan and drizzle 2× 15ml/tbsp olive oil over each one before baking.

7 · Bake in the pre-heated oven for 5min, then reduce the setting to gas mark 6/200°C/400°F for a further 5-10min, until the dough is lightly browned and the filling is bubbling hot.
8 · Serve immediately.

COOK'S NOTE: *Pizza oil is an olive oil flavoured with pimentos and spices.*

Further Topping Ideas: Pizzas allow you to show your creative genius – and to use up all sorts of bits and pieces lurking in the 'fridge! Try tuna, sardines or anchovies, or chopped spinach with plenty of garlic and black pepper. Any thinly sliced salami works well, also cold roast meat with garlic and chilli sauce.

Lemon & Pistachio Pudding
Serves 6

This pudding combines Ricotta cheese with Mascarpone, a sweet dessert cheese that is very rich. Use a good cream cheese if you cannot find Mascarpone.

225g/8oz Ricotta cheese
225g/8oz Mascarpone cheese
50g/2oz/¼ cup caster sugar
50g/2oz/¼ cup plain flour
4 eggs, separated
2 lemons, grated rind and juice
125g/4oz/1 cup pistachio kernels
cream for serving

1 · Lightly grease a 20cm/7in soufflé dish. Pre-heat the oven to gas mark 5/190°C/375°F.
2 · Beat the Ricotta and Mascarpone together until soft, add the caster sugar and beat until fluffy.
3 · Add the flour and the egg yolks and beat well, then add the lemon juice and rind and mix until evenly incorporated. Fold in the pistachios.
4 · In a separate bowl whisk the egg whites until stiff. Fold the whites into the cheese mixture, then turn into the prepared soufflé dish.
5 · Bake in the pre-heated oven for 40-45min, until the pudding is browned and set.
6 · Serve immediately with cream.

DRESSING UP

(l to r) Smoked Pheasant Salad; Fromage
Frais & Cranberry Dressing; Mixed Nut
Salad with Garlic Vinaigrette;
Smoked Turkey Salad with Stilton &
Walnut Cream Dressing; Smoked Quails'
Eggs & Mozzarella Salad

A salad of even the simplest ingredients is enlivened by an innovative dressing. If the salad is delicate, then a flavoured vinegar or aromatic oil may be sufficient, as for the Smoked Quails' Eggs and Mozzarella Salad (recipe p23) pictured on previous page and dressed only with virgin olive oil. More adventurous dressings might contain fruits or cheese. Avoid strongly flavoured dressings with delicate salads, but be bold and experiment.

RASPBERRY & HAZELNUT VINAIGRETTE

Raspberry vinegar makes a wonderful salad dressing but is also used extensively in nouvelle cuisine for sauces and trickled over soft fruits (sometimes with a little black pepper). Hazelnut oil is the secret ingredient of so many sumptuous French salads where its fresh flavour sparkles over the vegetables. Combine the two for a very special dressing.

75ml/3fl oz raspberry vinegar
75ml/3fl oz hazelnut oil

Place the two ingredients together in a vinaigrette bottle or small screw-top jar and shake vigorously until blended. Pour over a green salad and serve immediately or hand separately.

COOK'S NOTE: *This vinaigrette is unusual as it has equal quantities of vinegar and oil. This is because they both have such distinct flavours and the resulting dressing is more balanced using these quantities. I find that no additional seasoning is necessary.*

FROMAGE FRAIS & CRANBERRY DRESSING

125g/4oz/1 cup fromage frais
3×15ml/tbsp cranberry sauce
1×15ml/tbsp raspberry vinegar

1 · Place the fromage frais and cranberry sauce in a liquidiser or processor and blend well. Alternatively, whisk together in a bowl.
2 · Add the raspberry vinegar, which will prevent the dressing from being too sweet. Mix well.

COOK'S NOTE: *This dressing is especially successful with a salad of crisp vegetables and smoked*

poultry or game. The salad pictured overleaf to accompany the dressing is of sliced radishes, raw mushrooms, chopped pickled walnuts, orange segments and smoked pheasant. Smoked chicken or turkey could be substituted.

GARLIC VINAIGRETTE

This is a very simple variation of the basic vinaigrette dressing on p31, using a flavoured vinegar for added interest.

75ml/3fl oz/¼ cup garlic vinegar
150ml/6fl oz/½ cup grapeseed or peanut oil
salt and pepper
1×15ml/tbsp freshly chopped parsley

Place all the ingredients in a vinaigrette bottle or small screw-top jar and shake vigorously until blended. Use immediately.

COOK'S NOTE: *The garlic vinaigrette is pictured overleaf as a dressing for a mixed nut salad. Combine 125g/4oz salted cashew nuts, 125g/4oz chopped walnuts and 125g/4oz pistachio kernels with two red and two green eating apples, peeled, finely diced and tossed in lemon juice. Pour the garlic vinaigrette over and toss the salad, then serve immediately, scattered with cress. If left to stand, the flavours will combine but the nuts may become slightly soft.*

STILTON & WALNUT CREAM DRESSING

This recipe produces a thick, creamy dressing. Add a little mayonnaise if a thinner consistency is required, or use single cream instead of double.

125g/4oz/1 cup Stilton cheese, crumbled
salt and freshly ground black pepper
125ml/5fl oz/⅔ cup double or thick cream
75ml/3fl oz/¼ cup walnut oil
crumbled Stilton to garnish

Place all the ingredients in a liquidiser or food processor and blend to a thick paste. Season to taste and serve with the salad of your choice.

COOK'S NOTE: *The easiest way to crumble any blue cheese is to stroke it with a fork until crumbed. The dressing is pictured overleaf with a salad of smoked turkey, chopped avocado, lettuce and walnuts.*

OIL REFINERY

The use of oils in the kitchen has greatly increased in the last few decades, influenced by foreign travel and the subsequent awareness of international cuisine. Conclusive evidence of the links between solid animal fats and heart disease has also encouraged the use of oil, which now frequently replaces traditional favourites such as butter and lard.

There are many different types of oil, each having its own place in the kitchen. The best oils are generally the least refined, extracted without heat and left their natural colour. Such oils are described as 'virgin' or cold pressed.

Corn, sunflower and grapeseed oils are all for general cooking and are relatively inexpensive. Sunflower and grapeseed varieties are light and therefore particularly good for frying, leaving food crisp and free from grease. Corn oil is slightly heavier and more distinctive in flavour - I find it too heavy for salads. I use grapeseed oil for mayonnaise, finding that olive oil gives too rich a flavour.

Groundnut or peanut oil is similar in character and uses to sunflower and grapeseed oils but is rather more expensive. It is also a useful substitute for sesame seed oil in Chinese cookery.

Nut oils, despite their very high cost, are becoming more and more popular for special salad dressings where their flavours are superlative. Nut oil vinaigrettes are especially delicious served as a warm dressing for salads. Walnut, hazelnut and almond oils are the most popular. They are all cold-pressed virgin oils and should be kept in the dark and refrigerated after opening to prevent them from becoming rancid. Hazelnut oil is my favourite, but unfortunately is by far the most expensive.

Olive oil is the classic ingredient for so many fine dishes. Produced in many parts of the Mediterranean, the oil has been a major trading commodity throughout history, just as it is today. Olive oil is like a fine wine - you can buy 'plonk' for everyday cooking or an estate bottled vintage for the connoisseur. There are three common grades of olive oil: extra virgin, which is thick and green, and cold-pressed with an acidity of less than 1%; virgin, which is green and cold-pressed but with up to 4% acidity, and fine olive oil, for general cooking, which is heat treated during the second pressing to extract the maximum oil from the fruit and often blended with other olive oils. France, Italy and Greece are the major producers of olive oil and each oil has slightly different characteristics. Try them all to find the one that suits your palate best. I like them all, but tend to use the Italian oils most.

Safflower oil is very light and is used extensively in low-fat and special diet foods. It is rather expensive.

Sesame seed oil is used extensively in Eastern cuisine. It is a light oil with a high flash point, making it particularly good for stir-frying as it leaves the food crisp. It is also used to baste raw and cooked foods for extra flavour, having a distinctive pungency and taste.

Storage tips All oils keep best in a cool, dark place - ideally a larder. Do not leave your best virgin oils on display in a bright, sun-filled kitchen as they will quickly go rancid. Keep them in a cupboard, away from any heat source.

The more expensive virgin and nut oils are best kept for salad dressings and for adding to foods which require no further cooking.

VERSATILE VINEGARS

Vinegar is more than just a table condiment to sprinkle over chips. It is a product of fermentation and can be based on any alcoholic liquid such as wine, cider, sherry or beer. Originally used as a preservative, today flavoured vinegars are popular as condiments, especially on salads. A good vinegar is clear and transparent. Avoid non-brewed condiments, which are diluted acetic acid coloured with caramel and without the rounded acidity of a true vinegar.

Balsamic vinegar Very popular in the USA, this vinegar is produced by the acetification of grape must (new wine not properly fermented for drinking), which is concentrated and then aged in wooden barrels. It is used on salads and as a general condiment.

Cider vinegar Available straight or with honey, this vinegar is for general cooking and dressings for salads, including apples. It is a good substitute for rice vinegar in Oriental cookery. Cider vinegar is also thought to be beneficial to arthritis sufferers.

Flavoured vinegars Usually based on wine vinegar, there are many popular variations, such as blackcurrant for marinading and cooking game, garlic and herb for general table use, raspberry for sauces and dressings and tarragon for salads, especially on tomatoes.

Malt vinegar Based on beer and widely used for preserving and pickling, malt vinegar is also available as a strong, colourless, distilled vinegar which is particularly useful for preserving foods that have to last a long time.

Wine vinegars The most versatile of the vinegars, these are used for general cookery and in many of the classic sauces. White wine vinegar should be used for mayonnaise, Hollandaise and Bearnaise sauces.

Basic vinaigrette Vinaigrette is a simple salad dressing of oil and vinegar. It can be varied by the addition of freshly chopped herbs, mustard powder, lemon juice or garlic, or indeed by using a nut oil or a flavoured vinegar. The basic recipe uses twice as much oil as vinegar.

In a vinaigrette shaker or a small screw-top jar combine 100ml/4fl oz/½ cup oil, 50ml/2fl oz/¼ cup wine vinegar, salt, freshly ground pepper and a pinch of dry mustard. Shake until well blended. Use immediately. This will make approximately 150ml/6 fl oz/¾ cup.

BLACKCURRANT MARINADE FOR GAME PIES

Use this marinade for pheasant or venison. After marinading, add 2-3×15ml/tbsp blackcurrant vinegar to the meat during cooking and sweeten to taste with a little blackcurrant jam. Add a few mushrooms to the meat before baking under a pastry crust.

2 pheasants, quartered
* or 675g/1½lb venison, diced*
1 large onion, sliced
3×15ml/tbsp blackcurrant vinegar
3×15ml/tbsp olive oil
2×5ml/tsp pink peppercorns
1×15ml/tbsp freshly chopped mixed herbs
* or 1×5ml/tsp dried fines herbes*
6 juniper berries
pinch salt
2 bay leaves
250ml/10fl oz/1¼ cups red wine, approx

Place the pheasant or venison in a bowl or dish with the onion. Add all the remaining ingredients with sufficient wine to cover the meat.

Stir, then cover the bowl and place in a refrigerator. Leave for at least 24hr, stirring once or twice. Drain the meat and cook with fresh vegetables and wine. Allow the meat to cool, then top with pastry and bake.

(l to r) Garlic vinegar; sherry vinegar; cider vinegar; raspberry vinegar; balsamic vinegar; tarragon vinegar; vinegar with Herbes de Provence; vinaigrette

A Brief History of Coffee

The coffee shrub is a large evergreen tropical bush, originally found in North Africa but now grown in many areas of the world. It is found as far north as Mexico and as far south as southern Brazil. The best crops of arabica beans are grown at altitudes of between 2,500 and 6,000ft.

Coffee has been drunk in the Middle East for over a thousand years and its popularity spread rapidly throughout the world as explorers began to travel widely.

The most popular legend relating to the discovery of coffee tells of an Ethiopian mullah and a goat herd. The mullah, who was finding it difficult to stay awake throughout his devotions, was led by the Prophet to an encounter with a goat herd who had noticed his flock becoming very frisky after grazing on the berries of a certain shrub. The mullah made a drink from the berries which kept him awake throughout his prayers, and so began the tradition of coffee drinking.

Widely available since the 1930s, instant coffee is produced commercially by brewing ground freshly roasted coffee to a strong concentrate. It is then passed through an atomising spray into a stream of hot air to evaporate the water and leave a fine coffee powder.

Freeze dried instant coffee is more aromatic than the instant coffee powder and more expensive. The brewed coffee is frozen and then ground. The particles are put into a vacuum with a minimal amount of heat, which turns the ice into steam, leaving the ground particles dry and ready for use. Freeze dried instant coffee is always more granular and chunky than instant coffee powder.

Caffeine is found in varying amounts in coffee (and tea), and is a stimulant which acts on the nervous system. A small amount of coffee can be soothing and help relieve tiredness; it also sharpens the concentration. Large amounts of strong coffee can cause insomnia and, in extreme cases, palpitations and irregular heartbeats. Coffee is drunk at the end of a meal to act as a digestive stimulant.

Decaffeinated coffee is now widely available as beans or as instant coffee and is suitable for drinking by children and insomniacs and by people with heart conditions and high blood pressure, where caffeine can aggravate the symptoms. Coffee decaffeinated by chemicals is generally thought to be as harmful as the beans containing caffeine, so always look for the water processed decaffeinated coffee. The price of the product will reflect the process used, water processing producing a better quality, purer coffee at a higher price.

The best coffee beans are of the arabica type and are low in caffeine. Arabica beans are grown mainly in Brazil, Central America, Kenya and India and are the beans that are stocked by specialist delicatessens and coffee merchants. Robusta beans have a more neutral flavour, a higher caffeine content and are used in commercially prepared blends and for the catering trade. They are mainly from the West African coffee producing areas and Indonesia. Liberica beans, from Liberia, are prolific but have little quality or flavour.

Raw coffee beans are green in colour and have no aroma. Left unprocessed, they have a long storage life if kept dry. To release the aroma and flavour of the coffee beans, they must be roasted, the process which also gives them their brown colouring. The beans almost double in size during roasting. Well roasted coffee beans are always brown - black beans are over roasted and will have a bitter flavour and insufficiently roasted beans are pale and give a colourless, tasteless drink. As a general rule, the paler the roast the milder the coffee; darkly roasted coffees are more suitable for drinking black.

Once roasted, coffee will deteriorate quickly. Coffee contains volatile gases which must not be lost after roasting if the beans are to have a good nose. Many roasters now pack the beans warm from the roasting process in bags with a special filter which allows the beans to cool while preventing the volatile gases from escaping, taking much of the flavour of the beans with them.

If you wish to roast your own coffee, you should use the round peaberry beans from Kenya or Tanzania. These round beans, one from each berry, give a more even roast than the usual split beans and may be roasted in a single layer in a heavy frying pan over a moderate heat. They should be stirred constantly until they are the required colour. Crack a cooled bean and check that it is evenly coloured throughout; if so, the beans are ready for immediate use or may be cooled and stored in an airtight jar. Green peaberries are usually available only from specialist coffee merchants.

Hints on Making Coffee

* Grind the beans to suit your coffee maker, generally fine for filters and medium for cafetières and jugs. If your coffee beans are ground for you in a shop, tell the retailer how you brew your coffee.

* Use 4 level 15ml/tbsp of ground coffee for each 500ml/1pt/2½ cups water.

* Do not make coffee with boiling water. Leave the boiled water for 10sec before pouring it onto the coffee.

* Reheating coffee is not recommended as it can develop a very bitter flavour.

The Most Popular Coffees

Many types of coffee are grown throughout the world, each with its own characteristics. The following are the most widely available:

Brazilian The Santos coffees are the best, gleaning their flavour from the iron-rich soils in which they are grown. Bourbon Santos, the premier coffee, has a smooth flavour. Lesser varieties are good in blends. Brazil is the largest producer of coffee in the world.
Colombian Characterful coffees, rich in flavour with high acidity, Colombian coffees blend well. Excelso has a nutty flavour and Medellin is very fragrant.
Costa Rican These high-grown coffees with a fine, mild, slightly nutty flavour, are usually drunk with milk.
Ethiopian Wild Ethiopian coffee is spicy and blends well with a rich coffee such as Colombian or Javanese. Ethiopian Mocha is the name given to the cultivated Harar coffees, which are gamey and ideal for drinking black after a meal.
Guatemalan These mild, mellow coffees have a full flavour and fragrant bouquet.
Jamaican The most famous Jamaican coffee, Blue Mountain, is grown high in very small quantities. It is medium roasted to preserve its extremely mellow flavour. A great favourite in the USA and Japan, the demand for this coffee has led to its very high price. Two stamps to confirm the authenticity of the true Blue Mountain coffee have recently been introduced by the Coffee Industry Board of Jamaica to stop inferior coffees being sold as Blue Mountain.

Indian Mysore, a full-bodied, smooth, rich coffee, has a distinctive flavour on its own and blends well with Mocha.
Javanese The best Javanese coffees are strong with a fine acidity that is hardly noticeable. Javanese blends well with Kenyan, Colombian or Mocha coffees.
Kenyan are smooth, rounded coffees that drink well by themselves but are also very good for blending.
Mocha Usually produced in the Yemen, Mocha coffee has a winey, gamey flavour. It is a good after-dinner coffee, but is also very good for blending.

Coffee is also sold according to its roast - for example, French Roast is a strong dark roast while Italian Roast is a very dark or double roast. These continental roasts often have chicory added to them.

A selection of teas and coffees; the large cafetière on the right contains jasmine tea

34

TEAS & Tisanes

Tea is without doubt the world's most popular drink. Whether accompanied by a light meal of sandwiches and cake served in a cosy sitting room in front of a fire, or somewhere as elegant as the Ritz, a cup of tea is part of the English way of life and the tea ceremonies of the Orient are equally famed.

TYPES OF TEA

There are basically only two types of tea: green and black. Green tea comes from leaves that have been withered and dried immediately after picking to preserve their fresh green colour and light, scented qualities. These teas are mostly from China or Japan. Black tea is perhaps more familiar to most people; the withered leaves are left to fully oxidise (ferment naturally) to the familiar dark brown colour before they are dried.

CHOOSING A TEA

This may be to suit you or your mood or the time of day. The great thing about tea drinking is that so many varieties are available that you can always find a brew that is appropriate to the occasion. I like to wake up to a cup of Assam, a very robust tea, or a strong blend of African and Indian teas of the type that makes a good English breakfast blend; in the evening I prefer to drink Keemum or Lapsang Souchong. Teas should be savoured and the following brief descriptions may encourage you to try something deliciously different.

Assam Robust is certainly the description of this very big Indian tea. It may be just a little too strong for some people.

Ceylon A slightly fragrant tea of good character for all-round drinking. All teas grown in Sri Lanka have retained the name Ceylon.

Darjeeling Known as the champagne tea and highly regarded for afternoon drinking. It is grown very high in the foothills of the Himalayas and has a light grapy flavour, although I find it can become slightly acidic if brewed for too long.

Earl Grey Legend has it that the mandarin was so grateful to Earl Grey for services rendered that he gave him his secret tea recipe, to keep mind, body and spirit together in perfect harmony. As no tea

Tea in History

Tea is the leaf from the plant *Camellia sinensis* which is native to Assam, China and Japan. The bush is now grown in other tropical areas that have a sufficiently warm, wet climate.

Like coffee, legend surrounds the beginning of tea drinking and it is also reputed to have kept awake an ancient priest throughout a long vigil, stimulating him with its caffeine. We do, however, know that tea was valued and enjoyed in China and Japan for many centuries, long before it was introduced to India, Ceylon and Africa. It was brought to Europe and England in the seventeenth century, arriving on our shores from Holland via the East India Trading Company. The colonists in North America were encouraged to partake of the new refreshment but were taxed on tea and other imports from 1765 onwards, which led to a trade in tea smuggling from Holland to avoid the taxes. The East India Company later gained a monopoly to deal with the North Americans, but resentment caused the colonists to rebel against the traders and at the Boston Tea Party, the shipment of tea was thrown into the harbour by the rebels. Tea is not grown in the United States and, even today, most Americans prefer coffee.

Harvesting & Processing Tea

Only the top two leaves of the plant and the bud are harvested for making into tea. This is often referred to as pekoe, meaning the downy part of the shrub that is of the best quality. These have to be harvested by hand, like coffee, as mechanised picking would lacerate the plant and produce a much inferior product. The time of harvesting also affects the final quality of the tea, the best teas being collected during the peak season and the more standard teas during the remaining months of the year.

All teas are dried before use and are graded when dried - generally the larger the leaf the better quality the tea. The terms Orange Pekoe and Broken Orange Pekoe refer to the size of the leaf and not to chopped orange peel included in the pack!

was grown in India during Earl Grey's lifetime, it is obvious that this was purely China tea flavoured with oil of bergamot. In the past, many tea companies have included other teas in the blend, but more and more now seem to be reverting to pure China tea for this popular flavoured brew.

English Breakfast A strong, refreshing blend of African and Indian teas, although Ceylon may sometimes be included.

Formosa Oolong A semi-fermented or oxidised tea with a delicate flavour. It is difficult to find this tea, but it is worth looking for.

Gunpowder A green China tea of moderate flavour but with a spectacular visual effect as the leaves 'explode' in the pot to an enormous size.

Irish I am often asked for this but is is difficult to obtain. Basically, it is a very strong blend of Assam and Ceylon teas.

Jasmine A summer afternoon tea and known to many as the tea most often served in Chinese restaurants. It may be black or green tea flavoured with jasmine flowers, is very fragrant and is always drunk without milk.

Japanese I was recently given some Japanese tea to try. It is a large leaf green tea with a very delicate flavour, sometimes enhanced by the addition of toasted rice grains - delicious.

Keemun A most agreeable China tea for any palate and good with or without milk. It is weak but flavoursome.

Kenyan Dark and refreshing, it makes a strong cup of tea with plenty of flavour. African teas are also grown in Uganda, but the Kenyan variety is more often sold unblended.

Lapsang Souchong The most common of the smoked teas, it is smoked over burning bamboo roots. It is an acquired taste but very refreshing.

Flavoured teas These are becoming more popular and are generally Indian and/or African teas blended with fruit blossoms or oils, or spices. The most popular include apricot, blackcurrant, cinnamon, lemon and orange, passion fruit, peach and spice. They may be drunk with or without milk.

The Perfect Cuppa

* Tea is often dull if the brewing is rushed.
* Always warm the pot with hot water before making the tea.
* Tea should always be made in a china tea-pot - metal pots will taint the brew.
* Always pour boiling water onto the tea - freshly boiled water will always make the best drink.
* Tea should be allowed to brew for 4-5min - frenzied stirring of leaves and bashing of bags forces the flavour and emphasises the tannin.
* I always think that it is best to pour the tea onto milk in the cup as this distributes the milk more evenly - it also seems to produce a better colour.
* Sugar is, of course, a matter of taste but it can annihilate the more delicate flavours of green teas.
* I always think that it is better to make a fresh pot of tea than to top up the old pot.

Loose Tea or Bags?

For many years it was considered that tea-bags were filled only with tea dust, the fine residue left after the sorting and packaging of tea, and that the drink obtained by using bags was therefore of very inferior quality. This is no longer true and tea-bags are now available containing teas from selected estates according to the best crop available at the time of packing. These teas are unblended and have strong, distinctive flavours - one bag will often produce a pot of tea for two people. It is now a matter of personal preference as to whether you use loose tea or speciality tea-bags.

Decaffeinated Teas & Tisanes

Some teas are now available with the caffeine removed and these appeal to people who find ordinary tea too much of a stimulant, perhaps disturbing their sleep at night or generally upsetting their metabolism. It is not advisable to give tea to very young children because of the caffeine content.

Herbal teas or tisanes are also very popular with those who cannot tolerate caffeine. They are produced from flowers and other plants, are brewed with boiling water in the same way as tea and usually drunk without milk. Probably the most popular varieties are camomile and rosehip, but lime, mint, apple mint and mixed fruit are also easily available. Some of the best established tea companies are now entering the herbal tea market, offering blends for evening and morning drinking.

FINGERS ON THE PULSE

Many people wander into my delicatessen thinking that it is an up-market health-food shop. In many respects, my shop is just the opposite, although I certainly have a health foods section, as do many delicatessens.

In addition to dried beans and pulse vegetables, I stock several varieties of canned beans which are always very popular for salads and quick meals, where there is no time (or the customer forgot!) to soak dried pulses. I certainly sell more red lentils than any other dried pulse, probably because they are the only variety that does not require soaking before cooking and are therefore the most convenient. A delicatessen will usually also have a good selection of nuts - Brazils, pecans, pistachios, walnuts and cashews - all of which are invaluable in a vegetarian diet.

Lentils are either red, green or beige/brown. Red lentils are the easiest and quickest to cook; although the green or brown varieties have more flavour, they do require soaking. Red lentil dhal is a popular side dish for Indian meals, being rather bland and having the effect of cooling the heat of the curry.

Split peas are either yellow or green; the green variety is more difficult to find but has a fuller flavour than the yellow and is therefore worth looking out for. Both types are good in soups and for thickening casseroles. Chick peas have a deliciously nutty flavour and are excellent for vegetarian casseroles and salads, as well as being the basis for hummus, a very popular Mediterranean dip.

For bean cuisine there are many varieties, differing in shape and colour, but only very slightly in flavour. My favourites tend to be the beans that have a flavour of their own, especially flageolet beans which are a delicate green colour and have a subtle, fresh flavour; they are, however, rather more expensive than any of the other varieties. Mung beans are very small green beans that can easily be sprouted at home for use as a salad vegetable. The slightly larger burnished red aduki beans are nutty and combine well with orange in casseroles or salads. Haricot beans are surely the most popular beans in the world, as it is these that are coated in tomato sauce to make baked beans. Of the remaining varieties, red kidney beans are the most widely known, being a vital ingredient in chilli con carne, which strikes me as being second only to ham, egg and chips on the standard pub menu! This is all wrong, as chilli should really be made with pinto beans, a member of the kidney bean family. Pinto beans are a rather unattractive, dull brown colour, which is why they are generally replaced with the more attractive red beans. Pinto beans have the distinction of being one of the quickest beans to cook. Borlotti beans are similar to pintos, but a little larger and somewhat redder in colour.

I have made a selection of my favourite bean cuisine recipes that include dried and canned pulses. Some are main courses and some are salads. All are delicious and are well worth trying, whether you are vegetarian or not.

(front to back) Warm Bean & Mushroom Salad; Spicy Sausage Beans; Kidney Bean Tartlets

Kidney Bean Tartlets
Serves 4 (see p39)

The combination of a pulse vegetable and pastry provides a substantial supper dish. Eat these kidney bean tartlets with freshly cooked vegetables or a side salad.

175g/6oz/1½ cups wholewheat flour
75g/3oz butter or margarine
4×15ml/tbsp canned red kidney beans, drained
40g/1½oz Cheddar cheese, finely grated
125ml/5fl oz/⅔ cup milk
1×15ml/tbsp creamed sun-dried tomatoes with chilli (optional)
1 egg, beaten
salt and pepper

1 · Pre-heat the oven to gas mark 6/200°C/400°F. Lightly oil four individual quiche tins.
2 · Place the flour in a bowl and rub in the butter or margarine until the mixture resembles fine breadcrumbs. Add sufficient warm water to mix to a firm dough, then lightly knead and roll out the pastry. Use to line the prepared quiche tins.
3 · Place a spoonful of beans in the bottom of each tin. Sprinkle the cheese over the beans.
4 · Beat together the milk, sun-dried tomatoes (if used), egg, salt and pepper. Pour the mixture into the four tins.
5 · Bake in the pre-heated oven for 10min. Reduce the heat to gas mark 5/190°C/375°F and cook for a further 15-20min, until the quiches are set.
6 · Allow to cool slightly, then serve warm, or cool completely and serve cold with salad.

COOK'S NOTE: *Always mix wholewheat pastry with warm water to help the dough to bind together. Do not use breadmaking flour for pastry as it is far too coarse. Use a fine pastry flour or an '85%' flour which has the coarsest of the bran removed.*

Spicy Sausage Beans
Serves 4 (see p39)

This supper dish may be simmered gently on the hob or baked in the oven - yes, baked beans! It is surprising how many men enjoy cooking their own baked beans. It was one of the first recipes that my husband attempted in his bachelor days.

225g/8oz haricot beans
2×15ml/tbsp oil
1 onion, chopped
1×15ml/tbsp molasses
2×15ml/tbsp tomato purée
2×5ml/tsp dry mustard powder
2×5ml/tsp Worcestershire sauce
1×5ml/tsp salt
225g/8oz spicy sausage, eg Chorizo, thickly sliced
freshly ground black pepper

1 · Place the beans in a large bowl, cover with plenty of water and leave to soak for at least 8hr. Drain the beans and rinse well.
2 · Add the beans to a large saucepan of boiling water and boil rapidly for 10min. Remove from the heat and leave until required.
3 · Heat the oil in a large pan, add the onion and cook covered for 4-5min over a moderate heat.
4 · Drain the beans and add them to the onion with the molasses, tomato purée, mustard powder, Worcestershire sauce and salt. Add sufficient water to cover the beans and simmer slowly for 45min, until the beans are just tender.
5 · Add the sliced sausage to the pan and cook for a further 15min.
6 · Season the dish to taste and serve immediately with freshly cooked vegetables or a green salad.

COOK'S NOTE: *If you prefer to cook the beans in the oven, do so at gas mark 3/160°C/325°F for approximately 1hr.*

Borlotti Bean Salad
Serves 6

Borlotti beans look like dark-skinned pinto beans. Both types belong to the kidney bean family and have a slight nutty flavour. I have never seen dried borlotti beans but they are available canned and are very good in salads. This one is a particular favourite with my catering business.

1×400g/14oz can borlotti beans, drained and rinsed
1×400g/14oz can red kidney beans, drained and rinsed
6-8 small dill cucumber pickles, diced
175g/6oz cherry tomatoes
2×15ml/tbsp freshly chopped mixed herbs
6×15ml/tbsp vinaigrette dressing (see p31)

1 · Place the borlotti and kidney beans together in a large bowl, then add the dill pickles, tomatoes and herbs.

2 · Pour the vinaigrette over the salad and toss well. Chill in the refrigerator for at least 1hr, then toss again before serving.

Warm Bean & Mushroom Salad
Serves 4 (see p39)

Warm salads became very fashionable in the days of nouvelle cuisine. They make ideal starters as a warm dish always makes your guests feel that you have made an effort, yet they are very quick and easy to prepare.

1 × 400g/14oz can flageolet beans, drained
75g/3oz ham, chopped or shredded
125g/4oz cherry tomatoes, halved
50g/2oz butter
1-2 cloves garlic, crushed
salt and freshly ground black pepper
1 × 15ml/tbsp freshly chopped parsley
125g/4oz small button mushrooms
lettuce, radichio or spinach leaves for serving

1 · Place the flageolet beans, ham and cherry tomatoes in a bowl and toss together until well mixed.

2 · Melt the butter in a saucepan or a microwave dish, add the garlic and mushrooms and cook for 2-3min, until just soft.

3 · Season with salt and pepper to taste, then add the freshly chopped parsley.

4 · Pour the mushrooms and garlic butter over the beans and toss gently. Serve immediately on a bed of lettuce, radichio or raw spinach.

OLÉ FOR OLIVES!

(l to r) Black olives with Herbes de Provence; green olives with anchovy; Greek Kalamata olives; Manzanilla olives with almonds; Pork & Olive Casserole; marinated olives

Olives are grown in many Mediterranean countries, where they have been cultivated for centuries and have been an important trading crop since ancient times. They are either green or black, the green varieties being the unripened fruits of the same trees that produce the fully ripened black olives. Olive oils are described on p29, so I am concentrating here on olives for eating.

Many varieties of olives are available, either plain or stuffed with almonds, anchovies or pimentos. It is also possible to produce delicious cocktail snacks by marinating olives at home in a mixture of herbs and spices.

Olives are grown either to eat or to be made into olive oil. Most of the world's production comes from Spain and Italy, although Greece and France also grow large quantities. The Spanish influence in Central America is reflected in the wide use of olives in Mexican food and some crops are grown in Mexico and on the west coast of the USA. Like the vine, olives have recently been cultivated successfully in southern Australia.

Preparing Olives For The Table
There are very few varieties of olives that would be suitable for eating straight from the trees as the fruits, especially the unripened green olives, are usually very bitter. Green olives have to be treated in a soda solution to soften them before they are ready for pickling in brine. Black olives, being fully ripened, are naturally sweeter and are usually sold preserved in brine or olive oil. I think it is fair to say that the really top quality olives are usually sold in oil rather than in brine.

Prepared Olives
Olives are sold with or without stones, which are removed commercially by machine. They are most frequently stuffed with bright red pimentos, providing an eye-catching garnish and a good ingredient for adding to stews and casseroles. Also popular are almond-stuffed olives (although I always think the nuts suffer for being in the pickling brine) and those filled with tiny pieces of anchovy, which balance the flavour of the fruits beautifully.

Tips for Buying Olives
Green olives Mainly from Spain and France, the variety to look for is the Spanish Manzanilla olive which has a fine texture and flavour. Queen olives are larger and tend to be a little darker in colour and stronger in flavour.
Black olives These can be black or red, the red varieties coming from Greece where the best are the Kalamata olives. My preference in black olives are those from Provence, France, which are tossed in olive oil and flavoured with the herbs of the region - rich, strong and flavoursome.

Storing Olives
If you return from holiday with a large quantity of olives, they will survive longer if they are kept in a dark place, so that the light cannot cause any fermentation in the brine. Mould growth will also be retarded by adding a slice of lemon to the preserving liquid. I prefer to rinse the olives well if they have been bottled in brine and then to toss them in a little olive oil and leave for an hour or two before serving. Plucked straight from the brine, the flavour of the olives can be overpowered by the salt.

Marinated Green Olives

450g/1lb pitted green olives
2 cloves garlic, crushed
1 × 15ml/tbsp freshly chopped dill
3 × 15ml/tbsp olive oil
1 lemon, grated rind and juice
2 × 15ml/tbsp coriander seeds, lightly crushed

1 · If the olives have been stored in brine, rinse them well in running water, then pat them dry on kitchen paper.
2 · Place the olives in a bowl and add all the remaining ingredients. Leave for at least 4hr, stirring once or twice.
3 · Serve with drinks or as required.
4 · Store the olives in a covered container in the refrigerator. They should last at least a week.

Pork & Olive Casserole
Serves 6 (see p43)

25g/1oz butter
2 × 15ml/tbsp olive oil
1 large onion, finely sliced
2 cloves garlic, crushed
1,600g/3½lb boneless shoulder of pork,
    cut into 4cm/1½in dice
185g/6½oz can pimentos
200g/7oz pack pimento stuffed olives, drained
    (approx 125g/4oz)
400g/14oz can chopped tomatoes
1 × 5ml/tsp paprika
1 × 15ml/tbsp tomato paste
salt and freshly ground black pepper
sugar to taste, if required

1 · Heat the butter and the olive oil together in a large heavy saucepan or casserole dish, until the butter has melted. Add the onion and garlic and cook slowly, covered, for about 10min, until well softened and browned. Stir once or twice.
2 · Add the diced pork and brown on all sides.
3 · Remove the pimentos from the can and slice them. Add to the pan with the juice from the can, the drained olives, chopped tomatoes, paprika, tomato paste, salt and pepper.
4 · Cover the pan and simmer the casserole very slowly for 1½-2hr, until the meat is tender.
5 · If the casserole is still quite liquid, remove the lid from the pan and simmer more quickly until the sauce is reduced.
6 · Season to taste and add the sugar if required.

AN *ENERGETIC* CAPER!

It seems to me that few people have anything pleasant to say about capers, but I love them. They have a unique flavour and need only to be used sparingly to enliven the dullest of dishes.

It is a commonly held fallacy that the caper is the pickled seed of the nasturtium plant, although it is easy to see how this theory may have developed, as they are very similar in shape and are from a spreading plant of a very similar habit. Nasturtium seeds are edible and are known as 'poor man's capers'.

Growth & Harvesting

Capers are the unopened flower buds of the plant *Capparis spinosa* which has a low, trailing habit and grows abundantly in the wild, although it is cultivated extensively in Mediterranean countries, especially Spain and France, where the export of capers is a lucrative business. In the wild the plant is valued because its roots tend to anchor the otherwise loose soil and the autumnal leaf fall from the plants further helps the soil by fertilising it.

Capers tend to be expensive because they must be harvested by hand. The smallest varieties are the most prized, so the plants have to be picked over every two or three days to prevent the buds from becoming either too large or opening into flowers.

The capers are usually pickled in a white wine vinegar to preserve them. If the flavour of this solution is too strong, they may be soaked in milk before use.

Caper Berries

The Spanish are now promoting the use of the caper berry, the fruit that is produced after the plant has flowered, as a garnish for both food and drinks. These are fleshy fruits about the size of a small olive. We will have to wait and see whether caper berries take over when fromage frais and raspberry vinegar are exhausted.

Cooking with Capers

Capers are often used to garnish cocktail savouries and canapés. Added to a simple white sauce, they make a good accompaniment to plain meats such as boiled bacon. They also lend a delicious flavour when added to cheap cuts of stewing lamb with caraway seeds, especially if the sauce is finished by the addition of a little soured cream.

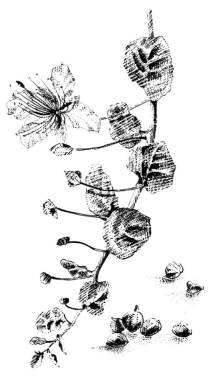

(*front to back*) Spanish Potato Salad with Capers; Skate with Black Butter; Lamb & Caper Pies; Tartare Sauce

Lamb & Caper Pies
Makes 4 individual pies

This is a very tasty way of using up any left-overs after a meal of roast lamb. Leeks always combine well with lamb and the addition of capers make these pies just that extra bit special.

40g/1½oz butter or margarine
40g/1½oz flour
375ml/15fl oz/2 cups milk
salt and pepper
450g/1lb leeks, sliced, cooked and drained
325g/12oz cooked lamb, cut into small pieces
2×15ml/tbsp capers
225g/8oz/2 cups plain flour
1-2×5ml/tsp caraway seeds
125g/4oz butter or margarine
water to mix
beaten egg to glaze, if required

1 · Pre-heat the oven to gas mark 5/190°C/375°F.
2 · Prepare a white sauce by melting the butter in a pan, then adding the flour. Cook the roux paste for a few seconds, then gradually add the milk. Bring to the boil, stirring continuously, then remove from the heat and season to taste. (This sauce may be prepared in the microwave cooker.)
3 · Add the leeks, lamb and capers to the sauce and divide the mixture between four individual pie dishes.
4 · Mix together the flour and caraway seeds in a large bowl, then rub in the butter or margarine until the mixture resembles fine breadcrumbs. Mix to a firm dough with cold water.
5 · Knead the pastry lightly on a floured board, then roll out and use to cover the pie dishes. Use any pastry scraps to decorate the pies and glaze with beaten egg if required.
6 · Bake in the pre-heated oven for 25min, or until the pastry is golden brown. Serve with freshly cooked vegetables or a side salad.

Spanish Potato Salad
Serves 4

450g/1lb cold boiled potatoes
400g/1lb can artichoke hearts, drained and halved
4 tomatoes, seeded and chopped
125g/4oz cooked peas
125ml/5fl oz/⅔ cup mayonnaise
125ml/5fl oz/⅔ cup natural yogurt
2×15ml/tbsp capers
salt and pepper

1 · Chop the potatoes into bite-sized pieces and place in a large bowl with the artichoke hearts, tomatoes and peas.
2 · Mix together the mayonnaise and yogurt and pour over the vegetables. Scatter the capers over and add a little salt and pepper, then toss all the ingredients together.
3 · Chill, then serve as required.

Skate with Black Butter

This is the classic way of serving skate. It may be poached in water or stock, but I prefer to cook it in the microwave, then coat it with the black butter. For two wings of skate you will need:

50g/2oz butter
1×15ml/tbsp white wine vinegar
2×5ml/tsp capers
1×15ml/tbsp freshly chopped parsley

1 · Heat the butter in a pan until it is lightly browned. Add the vinegar and capers and cook for a further 2-3min.
2 · Pour the butter over the cooked skate and sprinkle with the chopped parsley. Serve immediately.

Tartare Sauce
Serves 6

This is a classic sauce to serve with fish. It is so simple to make that, provided you have all the ingredients, I cannot imagine why anyone ever buys the ready-prepared varieties.

125ml/5fl oz/⅔ cup mayonnaise
1×5ml/tsp freshly chopped tarragon or chives
1×15ml/tbsp chopped capers
2×5ml/tsp chopped gherkins
1×15ml/tbsp freshly chopped parsley
1×15ml/tbsp lemon juice or tarragon vinegar

1 · Blend all the ingredients together in a bowl and leave in the refrigerator for at least 1hr to allow the flavours to blend together.
2 · Serve with any fried or poached fish.

SALT FROM THE SEA

Salt (sodium chloride) is a flavour enhancer and is used in many recipes, both savoury and sweet. A pinch of salt is taken for granted in many cake recipes and is added simply to bring out the flavour of the other ingredients. Salt is effective by stimulating the taste buds of the tongue and making them aware of the basic tastes of the food being eaten. Although the seasoning of foods is a very personal matter, I believe that it is preferable to add salt during cooking to benefit the developing flavours and not at the table, where the tongue will distinguish the undissolved salt added to the food. Salt has received much bad publicity in recent years as a major contributory factor to heart disease, but the initial hysteria has now given way to the theory that salt in quantity will only be to the detriment of those people prone to heart disease from other causes.

Products labelled 'table' or 'cooking' salt usually contain chemicals and anti-caking agents to ensure free-flow from the drum in which they are packed, giving rise to famous advertising slogans such as 'Everyone knows Saxa flows' and 'When it rains, it pours'. The more natural rock, sea and Maldon salts are completely without additives.

Maldon salt is a trade name for sea salt from the many inlets on the Essex coast. All sea salts are produced in shallow beds where salt is deposited by the ebbing tide and most of the remaining moisture is evaporated by sun and wind. Each successive tide dissolves the salt and deposits more, forming pools of highly concentrated saline. The saline is eventually filtered and then heated in shallow pans to complete the evaporation process before the salt is left to crystallise. Sea salt is usually available in coarse or fine grades and is best used from a salt mill as a condiment. Unmilled salts dissolve quickly in cooking liquors. Rock salt is the land equivalent of sea salt, having been deposited when the sea covered the area in a previous age. It is mined, then washed, filtered and artificially evaporated before being left to crystallise.

Salt and pepper are the two most common seasonings in cooking and are taken very much for granted. They have been used for thousands of years, one of the earliest references to salt being in the Old Testament when Lot's wife was turned to salt in the desert.

The Essential Seasonings

SALT & PEPPER

Salt has been used for many centuries as a preservative, whereby it is left on food to withdraw the moisture present by the process of osmosis. The salt retains the extracted moisture, thus inhibiting the growth of bacteria which require moisture to flourish in the food. Before refrigeration, salting was about the only process reliable enough to preserve meat. The same principle is still used, to a lesser degree, where vegetables containing bitter juices, such as aubergines and courgettes, are sprinkled with salt and then left until the juices have been drawn from the flesh. Vegetables treated in this way must be washed very thoroughly before use to remove both the extracted juices and the surplus salt.

Saltpetre, or potassium nitrate, is a preserving salt usually available only at a chemist's or pharmacy and is most commonly used to preserve the pink colour of pickled or salt beef. It is used in processed ham and bacon; also to preserve the pink colour of the meat.

The mineral traces in unrefined salt can sometimes affect the foods with which they are used. The mineral to be most wary of is calcium, which can toughen some grains when used during cooking. It is most commonly known to affect brown rice and sweetcorn during cooking. Stock cubes should always be checked for their salt and calcium content before they are used with brown rice, and sweetcorn should always be cooked without salt.

PEPPERCORNS - VARIETY IN COLOUR AND FLAVOUR

Black and white peppercorns are well known to all cooks, but any good delicatessen should also stock green peppercorns, both dried and pickled in brine, and pink pepper berries. Some delicatessens will also stock a mixture of dried corns of varying colours - not always natural - which look most attractive in an acrylic peppermill.

Peppercorns, which are harvested from a vine-like plant some 3½m/12ft high, *Piper nigrum*, were originally grown in India and south-east Asia, although they are now widely cultivated in other tropical areas such as Madagascar and the West Indies. The peppercorn was valued very highly and was frequently used in trade between the East and the West. The term 'peppercorn rent' relates to the time when the spice commanded a high price, although such a charge nowadays is generally disregarded.

The stage at which the peppercorns are harvested from the vine decides their colour.

Black peppercorns are the unripe, green berries which have been allowed to dry and blacken in the sun after picking. My favourite black pepper is the telicherry berry, which is hot and pungent and excellent for general cooking and for use whole in marinades.

Green, or unripe, peppercorns are available both commercially dried and pickled in brine. The latter are the hottest, the dried berries having a more subtle flavour. Green peppercorns can be used in place of the more traditional black for Steak au poivre, and also look most attractive when used sparingly with fish.

White pepper is milder than black and is best used with fish, white meats and delicate sauces, where both the flavour and appearance of black pepper would be inappropriate. The white berries are obtained by rubbing the reddish-black skin from peppercorns left on the vine until they are ripe. The resulting white peppercorn is then dried.

Pink pepperberries are not true peppercorns. They should not be used in any quantity as they can cause stomach upsets, but are extremely useful for the presentation of nouvelle cuisine dishes. They are purchased in brine and are less pungent and slightly sweeter than true peppercorns. I find them useful for flavouring game pies.

Mixed peppercorns look attractive and combine a variety of flavours and heats. They are sometimes mixed with other spices, such as allspice or coriander seeds, for a table condiment. Plain mixed peppercorns make an excellent flavouring for venison.

50

Venison with Mixed Peppercorns
Serves 6

675g/1½lb venison, boned forequarter, diced

MARINADE
1 large onion, sliced
2×15ml/tbsp olive oil
2×15ml/tbsp red wine or blackcurrant vinegar
4 juniper berries
4 black peppercorns
4 white peppercorns
4 green peppercorns
1 bay leaf
250ml/10fl oz/1¼ cups red wine, approx

CASSEROLE
2×15ml/tbsp olive oil
1 large onion, finely sliced
225g/8oz green bacon, diced
25g/1oz wholewheat flour
bay leaf
4 black peppercorns
4 white peppercorns
4 green peppercorns
2×15ml/tbsp tomato purée
250ml/10fl oz/1¼ cups red wine
2×15ml/tbsp redcurrant jelly
salt
1×15ml/tbsp Demerara sugar
freshly chopped parsley to garnish

1 · Place the venison in a large bowl with all the ingredients for the marinade. Stir well and add sufficient red wine to cover the meat. Cover and leave in the refrigerator for at least 24hr, stirring occasionally. Drain the meat from the marinade.
2 · Heat the oil in a large casserole dish or saucepan, add the onion, cover and cook over a moderate heat until softened and transparent, about 5min.
3 · Add the bacon and venison and cook quickly for a few minutes, stirring frequently, to seal the meat.
4 · Sprinkle the flour into the pan and stir thoroughly. Add all the remaining ingredients except the redcurrant jelly and sugar. Add sufficient wine to cover the ingredients. Cover and cook in the pre-heated oven for 3½-4hr, until the venison is cooked and tender.
5 · Add the redcurrant jelly and season to taste with salt and sugar.
6 · Serve the venison, garnished with freshly chopped parsley.

Steak au Poivre
Serves 2

Steak au poivre is traditionally served in a rich sauce of brandy and cream. This recipe gives the option of choosing the traditional sauce, or one using green peppercorns, red wine and yogurt for a lighter but very hot variation.

2 steaks, size and cut to suit your pocket
2-3×15ml/tbsp olive oil
3×5ml/tsp black peppercorns
2×15ml/tbsp brandy
125ml/5fl oz/⅔ cup double or thick cream
salt

1 · Brush the steaks with the oil. Crush the peppercorns coarsely, then press into the surface of the steaks. Leave the meat for as long as possible before cooking.
2 · Heat a large, heavy frying-pan on the hob. Brown the steaks quickly on both sides, then cook to the required state. No extra fat should be required to stop the steaks from sticking to the pan.
3 · Transfer the meat to warmed plates. Add the brandy to the meat juices and heat for a few seconds before igniting. Allow the flames to die down with the pan off the heat.
4 · Slowly stir the cream into the pan, then heat gently until warm, but do not allow the cream to boil. Season to taste with salt, then serve over the steaks.

To vary, used drained green peppercorns in brine. After cooking these steaks, add 125ml/5fl oz/⅔ cup red wine to the pan, then boil rapidly until the wine is well reduced. Remove the pan from the heat and stir 2×15ml/tbsp strained Greek yogurt into the sauce. Whisk until the yogurt is incorporated, season with salt, then serve over the steaks.

FAR EASTERN

Supermarket and delicatessen shelves are often stocked with many interesting tins and bottles of sauces that conjure up the promise of the Orient with their exotic names. To attempt to summarise the cookery of the Far East in two or three paragraphs would be impossible, so I will limit myself to a brief description of some of the more readily available Oriental foods, and an Eastern style recipe for the buffet table which is always very popular in my catering business.

Bamboo shoots After water chestnuts, I think these are the most successful of the canned vegetables for Oriental cookery. They are flat strips cut from young shoots of the bamboo plant and can be eaten straight from the tin or stir fried.

Bean sprouts The canned variety tends to be mushy and should therefore be avoided. This is the one unusual Chinese vegetable that is available fresh almost everywhere.

Black beans These are used in many Eastern dishes, either whole or made into a sauce. Black beans are used extensively in Cantonese cookery and are usually served with fish or beef. They are fermented and, consequently, have a strong flavour, being mixed with soya sauce and salt. The sauce is milder than the canned beans.

Chinese egg noodles These are used in many Oriental dishes, but are also useful for store-cupboard cookery. The noodles are very thin and simply require boiling water to be poured over them and should then be left to steep for 3-4min. They can be added to stir-fry vegetables at the end of cooking or served as an accompaniment.

Hoisin A Chinese barbecue, sweet and sour sauce.

Ketjap manis A sweet soya sauce used in Indonesian cookery.

Mie noodles Flat egg noodles, similar to egg pasta, mie noodles cook quickly and have a good flavour and texture. They are particularly favoured for Indonesian and Thai cookery, but are used throughout the Orient.

PROMISE

Sambals The Oriental equivalent to chutneys, sambals are strong relishes for serving with Oriental foods, often based on amazingly hot peppers.

Soya sauce A thin salty sauce used as the main condiment throughout the Far East, virtually replacing dry salt. It is made from fermented soya beans and the whole process of producing the sauce should take at least a year. Lesser sauces have sugar added to speed the fermentation process, so look for tamari, which is always naturally fermented. Other grains and flakes can be added to the basic sauce during fermentation for extra flavour - for example, wheat and soya-bean flakes are added to shoyu. All soya sauces provide invaluable seasoning to strict vegetarian diets that are based mainly on relatively bland grains.

Teriyaki A marinade based on soya sauce but with the addition of Tabasco sauce, sherry and sugar. It is rounder and more pungent than soya sauce.

Tofu Widely used in Eastern cookery and in strict vegetarian diets in other parts of the world, tofu is bean curd and can be eaten cold or cooked in a number of ways. It is a valuable vegetable protein. Tofu is available fresh or in long-life packs; the fresh variety has a firmer texture.

Water chestnuts A tuber, similar to Jerusalem artichokes in habit, that is grown in the East Indies, China and Japan. Water chestnuts are very crisp and are used for texture as much as flavour. They are sold canned but, being dense in texture, do not lose their crispness, even when cooked.

COOKING WITH A WOK

The wok is used for the majority of Eastern cookery. It has sloping sides and a small base to allow maximum heat over the maximum possible surface area, thus encouraging quick and even cooking. Woks are best used over a gas flame.

The very best oil to use in a wok is sesame oil which is pungent and flavoursome. The best alternative is peanut oil which is light but fairly full-flavoured.

Cook food in the base of the wok, and then pull the food up the sides to keep warm whilst adding more to the base of the pan.

Oriental Beef
Serves 20 as part of a buffet (opposite)

This provides an excellent contrast to the more usual turkey and chicken dishes to be found on cold buffet tables, in much the same way as pastrami enlivens a plate of cold sliced meats. Oriental Beef is very strongly flavoured and your guests will not require very much of it. It is stunning to look at and should be served cold with a rice salad.

1,350g/3lb cooked beef, thickly sliced and cut
  into strips
250ml/10fl oz/1¼ cups teriyaki
4×15ml/tbsp sesame or peanut oil
2 red peppers, seeded and cut into strips
2 green peppers, seeded and cut into strips
1 large bunch spring onions, finely chopped
1×170g/6oz can black beans

1×225g/8oz can water chestnuts, drained
1×225g/8oz can bamboo shoots, drained
1×400g/14oz can baby corn cobs, drained and
  halved if necessary
lettuce, spring onions and radishes, cut deeply
  and steeped in cold water to open, to serve

1 · Toss the beef in the teriyaki in a large bowl and leave to marinade for 1-2hr.
2 · Heat the oil in a large pan and cook the pepper strips and spring onions until just cooked but still crisp. Allow to cool.
3 · Combine all the ingredients in a large bowl the teriyaki will provide a sauce for the dish.
4 · Serve the Oriental Beef on a bed of lettuce on large platters and garnish with spring onions and radish waterlilies. Chill until required.

The Rice Bowl

Rice is one of the most important foods in the world, providing the basic diet of many thousands of people in the countries in which it is grown. It is thought that rice was first cultivated in India and Indo-China, but it is now grown extensively throughout the Far East. Smaller quantities are produced elsewhere, such as in the southern states of North America and Italy. The main requirement for growing rice is a lush wetland with extensive irrigation systems. In some areas, such as Bali, the cultivation of rice has been linked to religious ceremony for hundreds of years, to ensure an adequate water supply throughout the growing season. In the Far East it is said that a girl is not eligible for marriage until she can cook a perfect bowl of rice.

TYPES OF RICE

Eating habits in the West have changed dramatically during the last ten to twenty years. Just as white bread was once eaten in preference to brown, so white rice was always the standard choice. However, with the move towards less processed foods, the brown, unpolished grains of rice are becoming more popular, just as brown or wholemeal flour is favoured over white.

Whole rice is protected by an outer husk, which is always removed. The remaining rice in its unprocessed state still contains the bran and this is brown rice. Once the bran has been removed by milling, the rice assumes a polished appearance and is generally white in colour.

There are many thousands of varieties of rice, but they are divided into two main groups - long and short grain. Long grains usually cook up to give a dry, fluffy dish, whereas the shorter grains cook wet or sticky and have a tendency to cling together. Although it is normal to be served long grain rice at a Chinese restaurant, it is much easier to eat the shorter grains with chopsticks.

Long grain rice is the name generally applied to rice of varying quality and sold as an all-purpose grain. Always wash this rice thoroughly in a sieve under running water otherwise you will get a scum on the water in the pan, causing the rice to boil over on the hob and resulting in an unpleasant appearance when the grains are cooked.

Easy-cook rice is par-boiled to remove the surface starch that causes the problems when cooking other long grain rices. It is certainly easy to prepare, but I always think it lacks the flavour of some other types of rice.

Basmati is the everyday luxury rice. It is grown on the slopes of the Himalayas in Pakistan and has very thin grains and a surprising fragrance. It has always been acknowledged as a superior rice and with the move to whole grains, brown Basmati is now much in demand. This rice is not always easy to obtain, although it is now available in larger supermarkets. I use basmati whenever I can, and for dishes such as Chicken Pilaf it is superb.

Arborio or risotto rice is sometimes referred to as Italian rice, and is really a short grain rice, although slightly longer than the traditional round grain pudding rice. It does cook up wet and sticky, but has a texture of its own and is full of flavour. Arborio rice is grown in Italy and should always be washed before cooking.

Short grain or pudding rice is almost round and slightly sweeter than long grain rices. Brown or polished grains are available, the latter being the most common. I always remember making a particularly unsuccessful pudding with brown rice as a young bride - we ate chewy rice in slightly reduced buttery milk! Nowadays, I usually use the polished variety.

Wild rice is regarded as the most expensive grain in the world, and isn't really a rice at all but a type of grass. It is grown in swamp areas of the USA which are often very remote, and in Canada. The plants grow wild along the banks of the rivers and inlets and the grains are harvested from a boat. This takes a long time and is reflected in the price of the product. Wild rice has a very nutty flavour and takes a long time to cook. I think it has a fragrance reminiscent of Darjeeling tea while it is simmering. Wild rice is far too expensive to serve, like traditional rice, as an accompaniment to other dishes. It can be mixed with basmati rice to give an attractive appearance, but it is generally used for stuffings for game. The recipe for Wild Rice & Mushroom Stuffing complements pheasant particularly well.

Chicken Pilaf
Serves 10-12

Pilafs and other rice-based dishes are a very good way of entertaining plenty of people without too much fuss and expenditure. I prefer a pilaf to a risotto for parties. Although risotto rice always cooks up wet, your guests might think that something has gone wrong. A pilaf may be prepared in advance and heated through when required in the oven or microwave. Cut all the vegetables finely so that the dish can be eaten easily with just a fork.

675g/1½lb/3 cups basmati rice
3 pinches or sachets powdered saffron
1 litre/3pt/7½ cups water or chicken stock
50g/2oz butter or margarine
1 large onion, finely sliced
3 stalks celery, finely sliced
2 green peppers, seeded and cut into strips
325-450g/12-16oz cooked chicken, shredded or diced
175g/6oz/1 cup seedless raisins
1 × 185g/6½oz can pimentos, drained and chopped
salt and pepper
125g/4oz/⅔ cup pistachio kernels
freshly chopped coriander or parsley to garnish

1 · Wash the rice in a sieve under running cold water. Place in a large bowl with the saffron and measured water or cold stock and leave until required.
2 · Melt the butter or margarine in a very large pan, add the onion, celery and peppers and cook slowly, covered, until the vegetables are soft - about 10min.
3 · Add the rice and water to the pan with the chicken, raisins and pimentos. Season with salt and pepper, stir well and bring to the boil.
4 · Reduce the heat, cover the pan and simmer for 12-15min, until all the liquid is absorbed. Remove the pan from the heat and leave, covered, for a further 5min.
5 · Season the pilaf to taste with extra salt and pepper, then serve, garnished with freshly chopped coriander or parsley.

COOK'S NOTE: Soaking the rice before cooking in the measured water helps to produce a fluffier risotto of a richer saffron-yellow colour.

Risotto Milanese
Serves 6-8

This is a classic Italian risotto and is always served with Osso Bucco. It can also be eaten as a supper dish with a salad. It makes a very good (if expensive) alternative to macaroni cheese.

40g/1½oz unsalted butter
1 medium onion, finely chopped
150ml/5fl oz/⅔ cup dry white wine
450g/1lb/2 cups arborio or risotto rice
1 envelope or ½×5ml/tsp powdered saffron
1 litre/2pt/5 cups chicken stock
40g/1½oz unsalted butter
75g/3oz fresh Parmesan cheese, finely grated
salt and freshly ground black pepper, if required

TO GARNISH
2 lemons, finely grated rinds
4×15ml/tbsp freshly chopped parsley
2 cloves garlic, finely chopped

1 · Melt the butter in a large saucepan, add the onion and cook slowly, covered, for 5min. Do not allow the onion to brown. If your butcher will let you have a veal bone, scrape the marrow from the bone and cook it with the onion.
2 · Add the wine to the pan and cook over a high heat, uncovered, until the liquid has reduced by half.
3 · Add the rice to the pan and cook until it becomes opaque. While the rice is cooking, add the saffron to the stock and allow to stand.
4 · Add the stock to the pan and return to the boil. Cover the pan and simmer the rice for about 20min, until the stock is absorbed. Allow to stand for 2-3min.
5 · Cut the remaining butter into slivers and stir into the rice with the grated Parmesan cheese. Season with salt and pepper if necessary.
6 · Mix together the lemon rind, parsley and chopped garlic and sprinkle over the rice before serving.

COOK'S NOTE: *The risotto should be wet and sticky - don't worry!*

Osso Bucco
Serves 6

This is a classic Italian dish that is not too expensive to prepare, using shin of veal rather than an expensive boneless cut. The addition of the sun-dried tomatoes gives extra flavour to the sauce. Osso Bucco should always be served with Risotto Milanese.

50g/2oz butter
2 cloves garlic, crushed
6 thick slices of shin of veal, approx 225-275g/ 8-10oz each
2×15ml/tbsp seasoned flour
1 large onion, chopped
3 large carrots, peeled and diced
3 stalks celery, finely sliced
450g/1lb tomatoes, skinned, seeded and choppped
8 halves sun-dried tomatoes, chopped
1×15ml/tbsp freshly chopped rosemary
200ml/8oz/1 cup dry white wine
250ml/10fl oz/1¼ cups boiling vegetable stock, approx
salt and pepper

1 · Pre-heat the oven to gas mark 3/160°C/325°F.
2 · Melt the butter in a large heavy casserole and add the garlic. Toss the veal in the seasoned flour, then brown quickly on both sides. Remove the veal from the pan.
3 · Add the onion to the pan, stirring well to mix with any flour left at the bottom of the pan. Cover and cook over a medium heat for 5min, then add the carrots and celery and cook for a further 5min.
4 · Return the veal to the pan, add the fresh and dried tomatoes, rosemary, wine, stock, salt and pepper.
5 · Cover the casserole dish and place in the pre-heated oven. Cook for 1½-2hr, until the veal is tender. Remove the veal to a heat-proof plate if it is necessary to thicken the sauce, and keep the meat warm in the oven.
6 · If the sauce requires thickening, boil it quickly in the casserole or a saucepan on the hot-plate until it has reduced sufficiently - it should be thick but moist. Season to taste with salt and pepper before serving over the veal.

Wild Rice & Mushroom Stuffing

50g/2oz/¼ cup wild rice, cooked
15g/½oz dried mushrooms
15g/½oz butter
1 small onion, finely chopped
25g/1oz wholewheat breadcrumbs
1×5ml/tsp freshly chopped sage
salt and pepper
beaten egg to bind

1 · Boil the rice in plenty of water until soft, then leave to cool.
2 · Pour boiling water onto the mushrooms and leave to stand for at least 15min.

3 · Melt the butter in a small saucepan and cook the onion until soft and transparent.
4 · Drain the rice. Drain and chop the mushrooms.
5 · Add the breadcrumbs, rice and mushrooms to the onion with the sage and salt and pepper. Mix well, then bind together with a little beaten egg. Use as required.

COOK'S NOTE: *Rice-based stuffings do tend to fall apart when they are cut after cooking. This is probably why they are particularly good for stuffing game, when it is quite usual for a whole small bird to be served.*

Mustards To Relish

Everyone has heard that the mustard giants make their money from the amount of the condiment that is left on the sides of our plates. There are numerous varieties of mustards from around the world, although Dijon in France is acknowledged as the mecca of the trade and is still said to produce almost 50 per cent of the world's mustard.

All mustards are made from three varieties of seeds: white, brown or black, the latter two being hotter. The word 'mustard' comes from the Latin *mustum ardens*, meaning burning must, probably because mustard powder used to be mixed with grape must in France. This would imply that the majority of mustards are hot, but it is only the English mustard that is really fierce. (Chinese and Japanese mustards are also said to be strong, but I have not tried them.) Mustard does have a preserving quality; the seeds are often used in pickles and chutneys while the flour is used in piccalilli.

Mustard seeds may be used either whole or cracked, or pulverised into flour. The pungency of mustard is only realised when it is mixed with cold water; salt, vinegar and hot water inhibit the flavour, producing a milder condiment. Mustard should be allowed to stand for a few minutes after mixing and before serving to allow the flavour to develop, but mix little and often the flavour will be retained but the pungency will soon be lost. To gain the maximum flavour, always mix mustard powder to a paste before adding it to recipes.

As a general rule, mild mustards should be served with spicy foods and hot, fiery varieties to enliven bland food. I wonder who first decided that we shouldn't eat mustard with lamb? It certainly never seems right to do so.

VARIETIES

English This mustard is made from a mixture of white and black mustard seeds with wheat flour and turmeric. It is sold dry, in powder form, which is generally stronger than the more convenient ready-mixed varieties. English mustard is sometimes sold with horseradish incorporated, but I find that the flavour of the extra ingredient is lost unless it is a very well balanced mixture.

French There are many types of French mustard, but the most popular are Dijon and Bordeaux. The less common Florida mustard is made with wine from the Champagne region. Dijon mustards are generally smooth and fairly hot, although mild compared with English. Bordeaux mustards are darker and milder and often contain flavourings such as vinegar or herbs, especially tarragon. Bordeaux mustard is especially good in salad dressings. Whole grain mustards have recently become very popular and the best known French variety is the Moutarde de Meaux. I like to add whole grain mustard to white sauce to pour over cauliflower (*see also* Kidneys with Dijon Mustard Sauce, p76).

German These mustards are usually from Dusseldorf and are similar to Bordeaux varieties, often containing herbs and spices. They are particularly good with cold meats. I have many happy memories of eating Frankfurters with lashings of mustard in Cologne.

American A mild mustard that goes hand-in-hand with the hot-dog and hamburger trade. These mustards are often sweetened with sugar. I sell a very popular Canadian mustard called Honeycup, which is actually sweetened with sugar and is delicious with any cold meats, but especially with smoked turkey.

FRUITS
of the vine

There has been a great deal of correspondence in the trade press and the media concerning the absence of top quality vine fruits from the shops. This simply is not true. All the fruits are available, but you must ensure that your local shopkeeper realises that you want, and are prepared to pay for, the best. The difference is amazing - full, plump fruits bursting with flavour.

Vine fruits - that is, currants, sultanas and raisins - are full of invert sugars which are readily absorbed and assimilated by the body and are therefore a good supply of immediate energy. Many mothers prefer to give children a small packet of raisins as a snack rather than a chocolate bar. These fruits were traditionally sun-dried after fumigation to remove any bugs and insects, but many are now dried by accelerated methods to cut the processing time and, therefore, the costs.

Wine is now produced in many areas of the world and the production of vine fruits has also been spread far and wide. The majority of the fruits are from California, Australia and South Africa.

Currants were originally grown in Greece and are the dried fruits of the 'Corinth' grape, a small, black, seedless variety. Many currants are now grown in Australia, but I find that the best are the tiny Greek vorzittzas, which are sweet and plump. Cheap currants, especially if they are used in too great a proportion to other fruits, are bitter and can ruin a cake.

Sultanas are dried white seedless grapes and have a sweeter flavour than either currants or raisins. Look for the Australian Five Crown Sultanas which are perfectly delicious. If you want to add extra fruit to a cake or pudding, add extra sultanas.

Raisins are the most variable of all the vine fruits - they can be small or large with various grades in between. Red grapes come in many sizes, with seeds or without, hence the many varieties of raisins, which are simply dried red grapes. My favourites are the seedless Thompson raisins for everyday baking and for including in salads and pilafs, and the larger lexia raisins from Australia, which are usually seeded and are ideal for special cakes and puddings. As a dessert or table raisin, the flavour of the muscatel berry cannot be surpassed.

OTHER FRUITS TO WATCH FOR

Turkish sun-dried apricots are superlative. They have so much more flavour than the fresh fruit and can be eaten on cereals, used for puddings and fruit compotes, cooked with meat (especially lamb) or made into jam. Commercially dried apricots are exposed to sulphur dioxide to preserve their colour, before they are dried in hot air.

Prunes are dried plums and the best are the pruneaux d'Agen from France. These are delicious by themselves, but if you use them for Devils on Horseback (see p112) your cocktail party will surely be an enormous success.

Candied peel and angelica are coated in a thick sugar syrup, then dried. Both are at their best when bought in large pieces and chopped just before use, either for decoration or in cakes. Always flatten angelica with the blade of a knife before using it for decoration.

Panettone
Italian fruited yeast cake

Panettoni are widely available at Christmas time, often with marzipan paste incorporated into the dough or covered with chocolate. Homemade panettone made with top quality peel and fruit has a wonderful flavour that justly rewards the rather long preparation time. The cake keeps well in a tin or tightly wrapped in foil and should be served sliced, buttered or with jam. Try it for Christmas morning breakfast.

40g/1½oz fresh yeast
3 × 15ml/tbsp lukewarm water
6 egg yolks
1 × 15ml/tbsp vanilla essence
grated rind of one lemon
½ × 5ml/tsp salt
50g/2oz/¼ cup caster sugar
225g/8oz/2 cups strong plain flour, approx
125g/4oz softened butter
50g/2oz candied peel, cut into small dice
40g/1½oz seedless raisins
40g/1½oz sultanas
25g/1oz unsalted butter, melted

1 · Sprinkle the yeast over the water in a cup and leave to stand for a few minutes in a warm place before stirring to completely dissolve the yeast. Leave the mixture in a warm place until the yeast starts to bubble.
2 · Scrape the yeast liquid from the cup into a large bowl and add the egg yolks, vanilla, lemon rind, salt and sugar. Add the flour gradually, beating all the time, until the dough is still soft and sticky but can be gathered into a ball. Add a little extra flour if necessary.
3 · Add the softened butter to the dough in three pieces, mixing it in thoroughly - the dough will become very heavy and sticky and will be difficult to manage when all the butter is incorporated.
4 · Add sufficient extra flour to make the dough manageable, then knead it thoroughly for about 10min, until smooth and shiny. Place the dough in a clean bowl, sprinkle lightly with flour, cover and leave in a warm place to double in bulk. This will take about 1hr as the dough is very rich.
5 · Pre-heat the oven to gas mark 6/200°C/400°F. Lightly oil a 450g/1lb loaf tin or a 15cm/6in round cake tin.
6 · Lightly knead the dough on a floured surface, working in the candied peel, raisins and sultanas. Do not over-knead the dough while adding the fruit or it will discolour. Shape the dough and place in the tin.
7 · Leave the dough in a warm place to rise for a further 20min, then brush with melted butter and place in the oven. Bake for 10min, then lower the temperature to gas mark 4/180°C/350°F, brush with more butter and cook for a further 30-40min, until golden brown. Brush with butter once or twice more before cooking.
8 · Cool slightly before turning out onto a wire rack.
9 · Serve sliced, with jam and fresh coffee, or with a well-chilled dessert wine.

Cheese is an enormous subject. Many books have been written about this topic alone and cheese is indeed as international as food itself. Few of the learned tomes that have been written are for the domestic consumer and contain few, in any, recipes to lighten the technical detail. I cannot devote a whole book to the subject, so my descriptions of the numerous cheeses available will be rather brief. There is no better way of buying cheese than from a specialist cheese shop, where you will be encouraged to taste before buying and the retailer will be knowledgeable, friendly and, above all, enthusiastic about his stock. When talking about individual cheeses, I have tried to mention only those that are available in the UK without too much difficulty - I see no point in being lyrical about a cheese that you will have to travel to London (or abroad) to purchase.

CHEESE

THE CLASSIFICATION OF CHEESES

Cheeses may be categorised in great detail according to fat content, milk type and the cheesemaking processes used. For ease of discussion, I will split them into four main categories: fresh, soft, semi-hard and hard. It is usual to add blue cheeses, sheep's and goats' milk cheeses as three extra types, in addition to the four main categories.

Fresh cheeses

These are eaten very young - less than one month after the cheese is made - hence the term 'fresh'. They are often (but not always) relatively low in fat and can be made from skimmed milk or whey. They are soft in texture, usually sold in a pot or tub, and creamy white in colour. Fresh cheeses have become much more popular in recent years and cows' and goats' milk varieties are now available in most good supermarkets. Fresh cheeses are used both as table cheeses and as an invaluable ingredient for cooking.

Cottage, cream and curd cheeses are probably the best known of the fresh cheeses of Britain. Cottage cheese is granular as it is skimmed cows' milk curds, drained and washed before being coated in a very thin cream. The fat content varies, so check the nutritional information supplied on the tub. If a recipe calls for Ricotta cheese, sieved cottage cheese is the best alternative. Flavoured varieties are available, but it is far more interesting to make your own additions to the basic curds. Curd cheese is a low or medium fat cheese, very similar to cream cheese but having a more lactic flavour. It is often referred to as baker's cheese and is, as implied, very good for cooking.

Cream cheese may be moderate or full fat content and is used extensively as a base for dips, for cocktail fillings and for cooking. I find it rather rich for eating as a table cheese, but a few spoonfuls stirred into hot pasta is delicious.

Crowdie is the best known of the Scottish fresh cheeses. It can be laced with herbs or garlic and has a rather sour flavour - butter or cream are sometimes worked into the cheese to give a more rounded taste.

Many continental fresh cheeses have now found their way to the supermarket shelves and to the specialist delicatessen. Among the most popular are fromage blanc and fromage frais from France, and quark from Germany. All have varying fat contents, so check before buying if you are following a low fat diet. The lower fat varieties make interesting alternatives to cream on desserts and are especially good with fruit. Although these cheeses are very popular in Europe (it is said that the average German eats 5kg/11lb of quark a year, accounting for half their cheese intake) they may become a passing fad of the era of nouvelle cuisine in the UK.

Of the Italian fresh cheeses, Ricotta and Mascarpone are the most widely available and the most highly publicised. Ricotta was originally a whey cheese and therefore very low in fat, but whole or skimmed milk is sometimes added to give a richer cheese. It is usually made from cows' milk but the whey resulting from the making of Pecorino, a hard sheep's milk cheese, may also be utilised. It is used extensively in Italian cooking for both sweet and savoury dishes. Ricotta has a very short life and should be bought and used daily. This is not always possible outside large Italian communities and 'long-life' Ricotta, which lasts several weeks, is now available, but the flavour does suffer from this treatment. Mascarpone is the fresh cheese that really rebels against being low fat - it is virtually solidified cream. In Italy it is often found flavoured with crystallised fruits for eating as a dessert cheese, or it can be used plain for cooking, but mainly for desserts. It is also very popular as a speciality cheese; in layers either with Dolcelatte or Gorgonzola, it looks and tastes delicious.

(overleaf: *l to r*) Munster; Farmhouse Brie; Roquefort; Vieux Pané; Banon d'Or; Chaumes; Rambol aux Noix; (*in basket*) Vignotte; Pipo Creme

Soft Cheese

Of all the soft cheeses, Brie and Camembert must surely be the most popular. The citing of these two varieties will illustrate the basic characteristics of the cheeses of this type - uncut curds treated very gently and never pressed, the whey being allowed to drain naturally. Some soft cheeses are of the washed rind variety. This means that the rinds are dipped or rubbed with salt during their ripening period. It is more usual to wash or dip the cheeses in liquid. It may be brine or alcohol and this turns the cheese into what one of my customers calls 'garage cheese' - smelly! Don't be put off, though, as the actual rind of these cheeses is seldom eaten and the remaining paste is often surprisingly mild.

The French are the undisputed kings of the soft cheese market, but they must fight to keep the unpasteurised, fuller flavour Bries and Camemberts in full and regular production if they are to avoid losing the truly classic cheeses of their country.

Brie and Camembert are best bought from a cheese shop. Supermarkets seldom have time to nurture the cheese to full maturity and it is often sold with a large, hard 'chalk' in the centre of the paste, which is flavourless and most unpleasant to eat. Once a Brie has been cut in that state, it will seldom ripen properly. France, Germany and now the UK all produce Bries, although I think that the French varieties remain the best. Many additions are made to the basic cheeses, such as mushrooms, peppercorns, garlic and herbs, but the greatest distinguishing factor between one Brie and the next is whether it is made with pasteurised or fresh, untreated milk. Both have a good flavour when fully ripened, but the unpasteurised cheeses are very strong and an absolute delight! I do think that Brie is probably still unknown to you unless you have tried an unpasteurised variety.

Certainly the most successful of the 'modern' Bries has been Cambozola, a German cheese referred to as a blue Brie. It is a soft cheese with a Camembert mould on the rind and blue caused by the introduction of the Gorgonzola mould. When ripe, it is almost inclined to run, with a creamy flavour sharpened by the blue mould.

Camembert is also made from pasteurised or fresh milk and, like Brie, it is the mass-produced pasteurised cheeses that are the most readily available. It is, however, well worth seeking out an unpasteurised Camembert, handmade in Normandy and originally only available from the end of spring through to the autumn. Camemberts are still packed in the chipwood boxes that were first used for the cheeses in the 1890s.

There are many cheeses that are similar to Brie and Camembert but produced in different shapes or sold at differing stages of ripeness. All are referred to as surface-ripened, containing bacteria on their developing white rinds. Coulommiers is a small Brie, eaten very young when the surface mould is only just starting to appear, and Fongeru is similar but ripened in fronds of bracken and very difficult to obtain. Heart-shaped cheeses are also produced which are very attractive on a cheeseboard: Coeur de Neufchatel and Coeur de Bray are two of the best known, both from the Pays de Bray in Normandy.

Epoisses is a very popular washed rind soft cheese from Burgundy. It is usually dipped in white wine and develops an orange-red bloom on the rind. It is sometimes flavoured with peppercorns. Munster also has a reddish bloom to the rind and has a strong distinctive flavour - it is delicious on hot baked potatoes. Munster originates from the Vosges mountains of France, but is much imitated throughout the world. I have stopped telling customers that it used to be ripened under piles of manure, as it seemed to stop them from buying it. Pont l'Eveque is one of the oldest of all the cheeses made in Normandy and is distinguished by its square shape, being packed in small boxes similar to those for Camembert. It has an open textured paste when ripe and is usually washed or brushed with brine.

There is one very ancient soft cheese from Scotland that has recently been revived. Caboc is a cows' milk cheese made in small cylindrical shapes and rolled in toasted oatmeal to give it a more distinctive flavour.

Of the soft Italian cheeses Bel Paese, Mozzarella and Tallegio are the best known, although they are very different in character. Bel Paese was created in 1906 by Galbani and is sweet and buttery; it is used mainly as a table dessert cheese. It is named after the book by Stoppani, whose portrait is imposed over a map of Italy on the foil packaging.

Mozzarella was originally made from buffalos' milk but is it now a cows' milk cheese. It has a distinctive texture which becomes stringy when cooked and is most famous served on top of pizzas or lasagne. Eaten raw in salads, it becomes more interesting if it is topped with herbs and a good quality olive oil. If you purchase Mozzarella at the supermarket, it may be in brine or be ready grated; it is difficult to grate but melts more evenly if you make the effort. Other Mozzarellas must be stored in their wrapping in water, which requires changing every day.

Taleggio is a wonderful cheese when ripe; the paste should appear creamy and supple and the rind should be pinkish-grey in colour and not cracked. Eat it in the sunshine with Italian wine.

Perhaps the most famous of the remaining soft cheese is the Vacherin Mont d'Or, made in both France and Switzerland on either side of the border. This is a spooning cheese and should be served by removing the top crust and scooping out the paste with a spoon - from the retailer's point of view it is quite difficult to persuade customers that the cheese is as it should be. If the cheese is cut, the paste must be restrained inside the crust - thank heavens for film wrap, before which glass or wood had to be used.

Semi-hard Cheeses
This is probably the largest of all the categories of cheeses and it encompasses many of the traditional British varieties (see The Great British Eight, p86) as well as continental cheeses such as Edam, Chaumes and Pyrenees.

The Dutch cheeses Edam, Gouda and Leiden all belong to this group, although they may be sold at varying stages of maturity and the older examples will be harder in texture. Edam and Gouda are both eaten as table cheeses and used for cooking, when they melt readily. Kaasdoop, the Dutch version of fondue, is made with a mixture of these cheeses, although the addition of some mature Gouda will add extra distinction to the flavour. Although the majority of these cheeses are made on a commercial scale, a number of farms still make unpasteurised Gouda which has the word *boeren* (farmhouse) stamped on the rind. Leiden is very similar to Gouda and is generally sold in the same yellow paraffin wax coating. I call it curry cheese as it is very heavily flavoured with cumin seeds.

Switzerland is famous for six cheeses, four of which belong to the semi-hard family, although they are sometimes referred to as hard cheeses. Emmenthal and Gruyère are the most famous, Emmenthal having the distinctive holes, a nutty flavour and drawing threads when heated, whereas Gruyère has a very few small holes, if any, and melts readily and evenly. Both cheeses are slightly unusual in as much as they are made with cooked curds that have been heated in the whey for about 30min before being drained. Emmenthal must have Switzerland stamped in red on its rind, whereas the markings on Gruyère are in blue. The holes in Emmenthal are the result of the lactic acid in the cheese undergoing a secondary fermentation owing to a slightly higher temperature in the storeroom at the beginning of the cheese's ripening period. Emmenthal and Gruyère are mixed together to make a Swiss cheese fondue. Appenzell and Royalp are the remaining Swiss cheeses in this group. Both have washed rinds and a firm texture and tend to have the washed rind garage-cheese smell, as described in the section on soft cheeses (p69). Appenzell is especially good for cooking. All these Swiss cheeses are made in wheels, the retailer buying a wedge-shaped cut of the required

(*front to back*) Blau Castello; Gjetost; Gouda; Cambozola; Rougette; Emmenthal; Parmesan; Gruyère; Leiden

size. A large Emmenthal wheel may weigh up to 80kg/200lb.

Norwegian Jarlsberg, based on an old recipe but reintroduced in the 1950s, is best described as a cross between Emmenthal and Gouda. It has a nutty flavour and similar holes to Emmenthal. Jarlsberg is very popular in the United States and is becoming very well-known in the UK. Norway also produces Gjetost, a sweet, dark brown, fudge-like cheese that should be pared or sliced very thinly. It can be used to accompany dishes of herrings and other pickled fish, and helps to offset the acidity of these foods.

Of the French semi-hard cheeses, Chaumes, Pyrenees, Gaperon and Port Salut are probably the most famous. Chaumes and St Albray are washed rind, garage-type cheeses, having a firm, even-textured paste that oozes when ripe. The flavours of both cheeses are less powerful than the bouquets. When buying, avoid cheese that is dis-coloured under the rind. Pyrenees is a mild cows' milk cheese, usually in a distinctive thin black rind. It is factory made and the paste has many small holes in it. Pyrenees may also refer to small ewes' milk cheeses that are produced in the same area.

Gaperon is rounded in shape and made from skimmed milk or buttermilk and often flavoured with garlic or peppercorns. Produced in the Auvergne and usually ripened for about two months, Gaperon is expensive. In the past it was often hung from farmhouse ceilings to display a person's wealth (the more Gaperons the better) and to indicate the size of the dowry of an eligible daughter.

Port Salut is a washed rind cheese of a fairly mild flavour, originally made by Trappist monks when it was referred to as Port du Salut. The modern commercial version is very similar to Saint Paulin. If you are in France, try to find some of the Port Salut that is still made by the monks - it has a more distinctive flavour than the mass-produced cheese.

Esrom, from Denmark, and Tilsit, from Germany are also popular continental semi-hard cheeses. Esrom is based on a Port Salut recipe and has a washed rind and big bouquet. It is usually produced in rectangles and is easy to slice and therefore very useful for smørgasbord. Tilsit was originally made by Dutch cheesemakers living in East Germany, but is now made throughout Germany. It is stronger in flavour than the traditional Dutch cheeses and has a texture punctuated with many small holes. It is sometimes available in supermarkets, pre-packed in slices.

Hard Cheeses
Of all the hard cheeses produced throughout the world, Parmesan must surely be the most famous. It is the essential ingredient in much of the best Italian cuisine, whether it is cooked in the dish, sprinkled onto the food just before serving, or eaten as a table cheese. The best Parmesan is Parmigiano Reggiano, which has its name stamped on the rind. The cheese is sold at no younger than two years and up to five years old. Parmesan is a scalded curd cheese, meaning that the curds are heated to 58°C (136°F) before they are pressed. It is a 'grana' cheese - that is, grainy. Owing to its high price, it is unlikely that real Italian Parmesan is sprinkled generously over your food in Italian restaurants.

Sbrinz, a grana cheese from Switzerland, is a

TIPS FOR BUYING & STORING CHEESE

* Avoid soft cheeses with discoloured paste under the rind or with a damp surface; these will probably be over-ripe. Conversely, avoid those with a hard chalk in the centre, as these are not ripe and may never ripen if they have been cut too young.

* Do not store various types of cheeses together unless they are individually wrapped. Wrapping cheese in foil is probably the best method of storage.

* Avoid any cheeses that look hard or discoloured around the edges and that are cracked or dry.

* Cheese should always be eaten at room temperature to allow the flavour to develop. Cheese stored at room temperature will quickly begin to sweat and become very strong. Store your cheese in a cool part of the refrigerator and remove it at least 1hr before eating.

very good substitute for Parmesan, being only approximately half as expensive. It is slightly softer but has a similar flavour. Sbrinz is sometimes cut from the wheel using a chisel-like cheese knife.

Provolone, another hard Italian cheese, was originally made from buffalos' milk (as was Mozzarella), but is now made from cows' milk. It is distinguished by its flavour, the cheese being smoked before it is left to mature. Provolone is always made in unusual barrel shapes and tied in cords, which are then used to hang the cheese while it is maturing.

Cheese is always classified into the above four main categories, but individual cheeses may be put into different groups according to the author's opinion. What really matters is the ability to recognise when the cheese has been properly stored by the retailer and when it is being offered for sale in prime condition.

The cuisine of France has contributed so much to the culinary traditions of the world that to attempt to summarise all that is good about French cooking in the space of a page or two would be impossible. A country that has given us countless cheeses, truffles, classic dishes such as *moules marinières* and cassoulet, champagne and, for many years, some of the world's finest wines, requires several tomes to do it justice. You have only to look through any cookery book index to realise the extent of the French influence on even the most basic of dishes and the number of French recipe titles is further proof of a lasting international legacy.

The Flavour of France

Many French dishes are basically very simple but may take a long time to prepare in the traditional way. Food and its enjoyment are very serious business and are not to be hurried. As with any quality foods, simple traditional French fare may require the minimum of fuss. What could be nicer than a summer picnic (preferably involving a bicycle ride) of fresh baguette, ripe Brie or Camembert and a bottle of vin de table?

There are many dishes throughout this book that use French ingredients or that show the country's enormous influence. Illustrated opposite are the classic Salade Niçoise and a delicious dish of lambs' kidneys, sautéed in butter and served with a sauce flavoured with Dijon mustard.

OPPOSITE
Salade Niçoise;
Kidneys with Dijon Mustard Sauce

75

Kidneys with Dijon Mustard Sauce
(Rognons à la Moutarde)
Serves 2–3 (see p74)

This dish, suitable for a light lunch or supper, needs only freshly cooked vegetables or a salad of endive to accompany it. Serve with creamy potatoes or boiled rice if you require a more substantial dish.

75g/3oz unsalted butter
12 lambs' kidneys, skinned and cored
3 small shallots or salad onions, finely chopped
125ml/5fl oz/⅔ cup dry white wine
50g/2oz softened unsalted butter
2×15ml/tbsp Dijon mustard
salt and freshly ground black pepper
2×5ml/tsp lemon juice
freshly chopped parsley to garnish

1 · Melt the 75g/3oz unsalted butter in a large frying pan over a moderate heat. Add the kidneys when the foam subsides and sauté them quickly until browned on all sides, in about 5min.
2 · Remove the kidneys to a warmed plate with a slotted spoon and keep warm.
3 · Add the shallots or salad onions to the remaining butter in the pan and cook until just soft. Add the wine and bring to the boil, stirring constantly and scraping down any meat particles from the sides of the pan. Boil rapidly until the wine is reduced to about 3×15ml/tbsp. Remove the pan from the heat.
4 · Beat the remaining butter until very soft, then add the mustard and a little salt and pepper. Drop small blobs of the butter into the pan, off the heat.
5 · Slice the kidneys thickly and add to the pan with the lemon juice. Heat gently for 1-2min, then season to taste and sprinkle with freshly chopped parsley before serving.

Salade Niçoise
Serves 4-6

This salad may be served as a colourful starter or be made into a more substantial lunch or supper dish with the addition of some potato salad on top of the bed of lettuce. Select the freshest and crispest salad ingredients and serve the salad immediately after it is prepared.

1 large lettuce, cabbage or Webbs, washed and dried
4 large tomatoes, ripe but firm, quartered
3 hard-boiled eggs, shelled and quartered
1×200g/7oz can tuna fish, drained and broken into large pieces
125g/4oz black olives
1×50g/2oz can anchovy fillets, drained
275g/10oz green beans, blanched and drained
6×15ml/tbsp vinaigrette (see p31)
2×15ml/tbsp freshly chopped parsley

1 · Break the lettuce leaves into small pieces and use to line a large salad bowl or individual salad plates.
2 · Arrange the tomatoes, eggs, tuna fish, olives and green beans on top of the lettuce and then arrange the anchovy fillets over.
3 · Spoon the dressing over the salad, then sprinkle with chopped parsley before serving.

COOK'S NOTE: Tuna fish in olive oil gives a better flavour to the salad than that in brine; when the sun is not shining, the latter is reminiscent of the South of France.

Chocolate & Cocoa

Chocolate is a most romantic food if only because, as a woman, one expects to be showered with delicious boxes of confectionery at every possible moment (husbands and lovers, take note).

Chocolate is made from cocoa which was originally grown in Mexico, although the majority of the world's supply now originates from West Africa. Other beans come from Brazil, but the finest cocoa is still from Central America. In its raw state, cocoa is very bitter, and the beans, once removed from the pods, are left to ferment to diminish the bitter flavour before they are processed. The beans are roasted (like coffee beans) to dry the outer skin, which is then removed to leave the cocoa nib - the important bit.

Cocoa butter, the rich fatty substance in the beans, is extracted from the ground nibs and this is the basis of the chocolate industry. It is the percentage content of cocoa butter that dictates the quality of the chocolates that you buy. Cocoa butter is blended with sugar and flavourings and, sometimes, milk powder to produce confectionery, or is further processed to remove the fat, leaving cocoa powder. The extraction process for cocoa powder was invented by a Dutchman, van Houten, in the late 1820s, and his family firm still produces the best cocoa powder (see p79), which has a very rich and rounded flavour. I find it very difficult to obtain a regular supply of van Houten's cocoa; it sells almost immediately, so if you see it, buy it.

Cocoa has long been associated with the Temperance societies and other groups who fought against the consumption of alcohol. As cocoa contains caffeine, it would have stimulated the Temperance workers on their way. The village of Gospel Green, home of one of my locally made cheeses (see pp93–5), was visited by cocoa-drinking Temperance missionaries, although few of the generation who received instruction are still alive.

Chocolate bars are available in many flavours, but for cooking I prefer plain dessert chocolate, which is mildly bitter, or the French bitter patisserie bars. I often mix French chocolate with an English dessert variety for chocolate sauces. Bitter chocolate may be added to meat sauces for extra flavour - it sounds odd but it is very good and originates from a traditional Mexican dish of turkey cooked with very hot peppers, the chocolate being added to slightly sweeten and round the sauce. With regard to powders, as a general rule cocoa should be added to mixtures that are to be cooked and drinking chocolate to foods, such as butter creams and icings, that will not be heated. If you are melting bars of chocolate which will then reset, for example a chocolate biscuit cake, add an egg yolk to prevent the chocolate becoming cloudy and dull in appearance when it resets.

Rich Chocolate Cheesecake
Serves 6-8

This is a most unusual and very rich dessert. Serve sparingly.

1×20cm/8in pre-cooked pastry shell or biscuit crust
225g/8oz cream cheese
100g/3½oz ground almonds
125g/4oz plain chocolate, broken into pieces
1×5ml/tsp coffee essence
knob butter
2×15ml/tbsp honey or golden syrup
50g/2oz glacé cherries, halved

1 · Leave the pastry case or biscuit crust in a loose-bottomed tin.
2 · Beat the cream cheese until smooth, then add the ground almonds and beat well.
3 · Melt the chocolate, coffee essence, butter and honey together, either in a bowl over a pan of

water or in a microwave cooker. Mix to a smooth paste, then add to the cream cheese and beat well. Stir in the chopped cherries.

4 · Spoon the filling into the flan case or onto the biscuit base and smooth the top. Chill until set (approximately 2hr), then remove from the tin and serve as required.

Italian Chocolate Biscuit Loaf
Serves 6-8 (see p79)

All chocolate refrigerator cakes are rich, but this is even more so. Serve in small slices after a fairly plain main course. Pour cream over the dessert if you dare!

225g/8oz plain dessert chocolate, broken into pieces
3×15ml/tbsp rum or liqueur of your choice
225g/8oz unsalted butter
25g/1oz caster sugar
2 eggs, separated
150g/5oz blanched almonds, finely chopped
12 petit beurre biscuits, cut cleanly into halves
icing sugar for dredging (optional)
cream to serve (optional)

1 · Line a 675g/1½lb loaf tin with non-stick baking parchment.
2 · Heat the chocolate until melted, either in a bowl over a pan of water or in a double saucepan, or in the microwave for about 2-3min on 100% power. Stir thoroughly, then allow to cool to room temperature.
3 · Beat the butter in a large bowl until light and fluffy. Beat in the sugar and the egg yolks, one at a time, then stir in the almonds and the cooled chocolate.
4 · Whisk the egg whites until stiff, then fold into the chocolate mixture. When the egg whites are properly combined with the chocolate, carefully add the biscuit halves - do not add any crumbs.
5 · Spoon the mixture into the prepared tin and press down with the back of a metal spoon. Be quite firm so that it forms a solid chocolate loaf in the tin, but do try not to break the biscuits.
6 · Cover and chill for at least 2hr.
7 · Invert the loaf onto a serving plate and remove all the non-stick parchment. Dredge with sieved icing sugar, if required, and serve in slices.

Black Forest Gâteau
Serves 10-12 (see p79)

Year after year, this is constantly the favourite dessert when eating out. If you take the time and trouble to make your own, you will discover a truly delicious gâteau.

60g/2½oz unsalted butter
6 eggs
175g/6oz/⅔ cup caster sugar
3×15ml/tbsp cocoa powder sieved together with
* 90g/3½oz plain flour*
6×15ml/tbsp kirsch
350ml/15fl oz/2 cups double or thick cream, whipped
1×400g/14oz can pitted black cherries, drained
Chocolate caraque to decorate (see Cook's Note, below)

1 · Pre-heat the oven to gas mark 5/190°C/375°F. Lightly grease and line 2×22cm/8in sandwich tins.
2 · Heat the butter until melted, then allow to cool slightly.
3 · Whisk together the eggs and sugar until very thick - you should be able to write a four-lettered word in the mixture.
4 · Sieve half the flour onto the eggs and fold in lightly with a metal spoon, then fold in half the butter, the remaining flour, then the remaining butter. Pour into the prepared tins and bake immediately, for 20-25min or until the cakes are cooked.
5 · Turn onto a wire cooling rack and leave until cold.
6 · Place one cake on a serving plate, spike all over with a skewer and lace with half the kirsch. Spread the cake with cream and then top with the drained cherries. Place the remaining cake on top of the cherries, spike and lace with kirsch as before.
7 · Spread the remaining cream over the cakes and decorate with the chocolate caraque. Leave for at least 2hr before serving to allow the kirsch to soak properly into the cakes.

COOK'S NOTE: *To make caraque, melt about 175g/6oz plain chocolate, then spread it thickly on some baking parchment and leave to set. Scrape a large sharp knife across the surface, shaving off rolls of very fine chocolate. Scatter these over the cake.*

Black Forest Gateau;
Italian Chocolate Biscuit Loaf

FASTA PASTA

Pasta is quick to prepare and provides a substantial, tasty meal without too much time and effort.

Pasta has been eaten in Italy for centuries and there are records of the ancient Etruscans eating laganon, or sheets of pasta that we now call lasagne. Pasta is the ideal mid-week supper dish and the possibilities for tasty accompanying sauces are endless. The following selection of sauces are all quick to prepare. Some are based on classic recipes and some on contemporary flavours and foods; some can be made almost entirely from the store-cupboard.

Basic pasta itself is made from a stiff dough of flour and water, although eggs may sometimes be included. The best pasta is made with durum wheat, a very hard, translucent grain. For wholefood enthusiasts, I would recommend buckwheat pasta rather than wholemeal, which I think is rather dull in flavour and texture. Buckwheat pasta has a strong, nutty flavour. If you are making your own pasta, use a strong flour, such as you would have for breadmaking. Homemade pasta requires a very definite skill which I haven't got (the texture of the dough is of paramount importance), so I cheat and use fresh pasta for special occasions. This is widely available in supermarkets and delicatessens. The quality of dried pasta varies enormously - always check that it is made from durum wheat. A plain flour and water dough will be referred to as 'pasta secca' while an egg pasta will be labelled as 'pasta all'uovo'.

Pasta comes in all shapes and sizes, some for specific recipes, such as the large sheets of lasagne, but many of the others can be used as required. Filled pasta shapes, such as ravioli and tortellini, make an instant meal with some prepared tomato sauce. The fillings may be meat based, or a mixture of spinach and Ricotta cheese.

I think that spaghetti should be thin and it may often be referred to as spaghettini - it's much less like eating long worms! Pasta may be flavoured with spinach (verde), tomato or carrot and tri-colour pastas are now widely available, which have a particularly attractive appearance. Of all the shapes my favourite is penne - medium-sized tubes of pasta that fill up with large amounts of sauce. If you visit the USA, do try to find some of the very large pasta shells that are available there - one of these per person makes a wonderful starter.

The following is a selection of my favourite pasta sauce recipes. They all serve four and are to accompany 500g/1lb dried pasta, cooked as directed on the packet. Vary the amount of pasta to suit your own appetite.

Creamed Leek & Chilli Sauce

450g/1lb leeks, trimmed, sliced and freshly cooked
1×113g/4oz can green chillis in brine for Mexican
  cooking
25g/1oz butter
3 cloves garlic, crushed or finely chopped
225g/8oz cream cheese
salt and pepper
1×5ml/tsp paprika
watercress to garnish

1 · Drain the leeks and place in a liquidiser or food processor with the green chillis and the brine. Process to a smooth purée.
2 · Heat the butter until melted in a large saucepan, add the garlic and cook for 1min. Stir the leek purée into the butter and cook over a moderate heat until warmed through.
3 · Stir in the cream cheese and continue to cook until thoroughly blended and piping hot. Add salt, pepper and paprika to taste.
4 · Drain the pasta and rinse in boiling water. Toss the pasta in the sauce and place in a warmed serving dish. Garnish boldly with watercress and serve.

COOK'S NOTE: A milder sauce can be made by puréeing the leeks with 250ml/10fl oz/1¼ cups milk instead of the canned chillis. Freshly cooked and puréed spinach may also be used.

Clam Sauce

3×15ml/tbsp white wine
½×400g/14oz can clam soup or chowder
5×15ml/tbsp olive oil
2 cloves garlic, finely chopped
2×290g/10oz can clams, drained
25g/1oz soft butter
2 × 15ml/tbsp freshly chopped parsley or 1 × 15ml/
  tbsp dried
salt and white pepper

1 · Boil the wine rapidly in a small saucepan until it has reduced to approx 1×15ml/tbsp. Stir in the clam soup and set to one side.
2 · Heat the oil in a large frying pan, add the garlic and cook for a few seconds. Add the wine and clam soup and boil quickly until the sauce has stopped foaming and is well reduced.
3 · Stir the clams into the sauce and heat for a further 1-2min until piping hot.
4 · Drain and rinse the pasta. Add the softened butter and stir well, then place in a serving dish with the sauce and toss them together with the parsley and seasonings until all the ingredients are well mixed.
5 · Serve immediately.

COOK'S NOTE: This clam, or vongole, sauce is traditionally served with spaghetti.

Quails' Eggs & Fresh Herb Sauce

24 quails' eggs, fresh or smoked or a mixture of both
25g/1oz softened butter
240g/8oz/carton strained Greek-style yogurt
2×15ml/tbsp freshly chopped chives
2×15ml/tbsp freshly chopped dill
50g/2oz pine kernels
salt and pepper
freshly grated Parmesan cheese to serve

1 · Hard boil the fresh quails' eggs for 3min, cool slightly and shell.
2 · Stir the butter into the freshly cooked, drained pasta with a fork, then stir in the yogurt. Add the herbs and heat gently for 3-4min, stirring constantly.
3 · Add the shelled eggs to the pan, stir well and continue to heat for 2-3min, until the eggs are piping hot - do not overcook, otherwise they will become rubbery.
4 · Stir in the pine kernels and season the pasta to taste with salt and pepper. Transfer to warm plates or a serving dish.
5 · Serve with freshly grated Parmesan cheese.

(front to back) Garlic & Walnut Sauce; Clam Sauce; Ragu Bolognese; Creamed Leek & Chilli Sauce

Ragu Bolognese

3 × 15ml/tbsp olive oil
125g/4oz smoked bacon or ham, finely chopped
1 medium carrot, finely chopped
1 carrot, peeled and diced
1 stick celery, finely chopped
325g/12oz braising steak, finely minced
125g/4oz pork leg steak, finely minced
225g/8oz chicken livers, finely chopped
125ml/5fl oz/⅔ cup dry red or white wine
375g/15fl oz/2 cups beef stock
2 × 15ml/tbsp tomato purée
pinch ground nutmeg
salt
freshly ground black pepper
4 × 15ml/tbsp double or thick cream (optional)

1 · Heat the oil in a large heavy pan, add the bacon or ham, onion, carrot and celery and cook over a moderate heat for about 10min, until lightly browned and well softened.
2 · Add the meats to the pan with the chicken livers and brown on all sides, stirring constantly.
3 · Add the wine to the pan, increase the heat and boil briskly until almost all the liquid has cooked away.
4 · Add the stock and tomato purée to the pan with a little nutmeg, salt and pepper. Bring to the boil, then reduce the heat and simmer the sauce, covered, for about 1hr - the longer and slower the better.
5 · Adjust the seasoning to taste, then add the cream, if used, and heat through, without boiling, for 2-3min.
6 · Serve with the freshly cooked pasta of your choice.

COOK'S NOTE: *The difference in flavours between a ragu prepared in this way, using beef, pork and chicken livers, and the accepted standard of Spaghetti Bolognese that appears on so many menus is outstanding. This sauce may also be prepared for lasagne, but omit the cream.*

Garlic & Walnut Sauce

125g/4oz shelled walnut pieces
2-3 cloves garlic, crushed
250ml/10fl oz/1¼ cups single cream
2 × 15ml/tbsp freshly chopped marjoram or parsley
salt
freshly ground black pepper

1 · Blend the walnuts, garlic, cream and marjoram or parsley in a liquidiser or food processor to a smooth, thick cream. Alternatively, chop the nuts very finely, add the garlic and use a pestle and mortar to grind them down. Add the cream a little at a time and finally add the freshly chopped herbs.
2 · Season the sauce to taste and stir into freshly cooked pasta, tossed in 25g/1oz butter and 2 × 15ml/tbsp walnut oil.

COOK'S NOTE: *This is a marvellous starter, divided between six or eight people and served with very fine bird's-nest or capellini pasta.*

HINTS FOR COOKING PASTA

* Always add the pasta to a very large pan containing plenty of boiling, salted water.

* Adding a little oil to the water prevents pasta from sticking together during cooking. (Using enough water is also important.)

* Do not overcook the pasta - it should be 'al dente' - ie, firm to the bite. Fresh pasta requires only 3-4min cooking, a much shorter time than dried pasta.

* Instead of rinsing your pasta after cooking, drain it and put it in a serving dish or back in the saucepan, then add a few knobs of soft butter. Toss this gently into the pasta to prevent it from sticking together.

* Except for the top quality, Italian-produced no-cook pasta, such products should be avoided as they tend to taste of cardboard and have a similar texture. There is always the exception to a rule: I sell an excellent Italian no-cook lasagne.

THE SOIL ASSOCIATION
& Organic Foods

Interest in the production of foods without the use of chemicals has been growing rapidly. Organic foods were originally mainly sought after by people suffering from various food allergies as conclusive evidence of links between many allergies and other problems and the use of pesticides and modern agri-chemicals was produced. Environmental issues now contribute much to an ever-increasing awareness of the overwork of the land and the pollution of the countryside. In an age where the ability of the land to produce more food than is required for many parts of the world is a fact of life, the argument for organic farming methods has never been stronger.

Organic farming is like wild gardening - you cannot just stop all planning and let nature take over. Striking the right balance requires a long lead-in period to allow the land to be cleansed of chemicals and to create a fertile environment through natural manuring and crop rotation. It is also important to realise that weeding of crops is manual rather than by mechanically applied chemicals, therefore taking much longer and being less cost-effective.

Most supermarkets now have organically produced fruits and vegetables for sale and the increasing choice of varieties available reflects the public's growing interest in these products. They do command a higher price, but the generally improved flavour, combined with an understanding of the increased effort required to produce the food, warrants the extra expenditure.

The organic food most commonly found in a delicatessen is cheese. This is invariably from small-scale farmhouse producers, using just the milk of their own herd, be it cattle, sheep or goats, fed on pastures that are organically fertilised with farmyard manure or a natural material such as seaweed. Very often such cheeses are made with a vegetarian rennet and natural sea salt. Any herbs that are added are also organically produced on the farm.

The number of organic cheeses available is constantly increasing and the varieties include hard, Cheddar-types, semi-hard and soft, creamy cheeses. It is very interesting to note that many people who have been unable to eat cheese because of headaches, migraines or digestive problems following its consumption are able to eat organically produced cheeses with no side effects.

The Soil Association exists as a standards body for much of the organically produced food in the UK. The well-known symbol of the Association is on all packaged foods that it recognises as being truly organic and indicates that the food has been produced on land that meets all the requirements of the Association. The Soil Association's symbol is the consumer's only guarantee that the food being offered for sale is truly organic and worth the premium that is demanded for foods produced in this way. At the time of writing it is possible that the organisation Food From Britain will assume responsibility for marketing and controlling organic foods, which may result in a new logo to certify organic foods.

THE
GREAT
BRITISH
EIGHT

— AND THE REST —

For many years the choice of British cheeses was limited to the Great British Eight: Caerphilly, Cheshire, Double Gloucester, Lancashire, Red Leicester, Sage Derby, Stilton and Wensleydale. These are, of course, in addition to the superb English Cheddar. Other varieties were made on farms in small quantities and were usually for home consumption only, but the resurgence of interest in farmhouse foods coupled with milk quotas that forced farmers to look for ways of using their surplus milk, has brought about a revolution in British cheesemaking, which is all to the good for the cheese eating public.

Cheddar is generally thought of as the all-purpose cheese, for cooking and eating. Available in varying maturity, it must be kept for two years before it attains a real 'bite-back' sharpness. Most good delicatessens should carry a one-year-old farmhouse Cheddar on the rind, and, in my opinion, this is really the only way to buy the cheese. Cheddars may be hard or semi-hard; they are pressed lightly for a matter of hours and then more firmly for a short period of days. This causes much of the whey to be lost, resulting in the firm texture of the cheese. Because Cheddar has been the yardstick of the British cheese industry, it has perhaps suffered more than any other of our cheeses, as it has been forced into mediocrity through extensive mechanisation of the various stages of making. It has also been shaped for ease of packaging, rubberised and refined, with the result that it is often quite tastless.

Caerphilly is the traditional cheese of Wales, although it was first made as recently as the 1880s. It has a slightly sharp flavour and is crumbly and moist. Processed

---

TIPS FOR BUYING CHEDDAR

* Try to buy Cheddar on the rind - it makes a tremendous difference to the flavour (like cooking meat on the bone), and instantly shows that the cheese has been cut from a truckle and not from a block.

* Any unpasteurised cheese will have a stronger, fuller flavour than its treated counterpart. Look for unpasteurised Cheddar.

* It is false economy to buy a milder, cheaper Cheddar for cooking. You will require much more to attain a good flavour and will therefore be raising your fat consumption for no good reason. A little of a stronger, if more expensive cheese, is much better for health, wealth and flavour.

Caerphilly can be rather bland, but a traditional farmhouse variety has a delicious, if subtle flavour. The cheese is only lightly pressed, which explains its slightly open texture. In Wales, Caerphilly was referred to as 'new cheese', as it could be ready for sale within ten days of making. Caerphilly is now enjoying a revival in Wales after many years of being made only in England.

Cheshire is crumbly in texture and pale peach in colour when young, although it darkens as it ages. Most Cheshire is eaten young, but it is quite delicious when matured. In addition to the usual peach-coloured cheese, there is a white Cheshire which is very popular in the North of England. The difference is only in the colour; the cheese tastes the same. Cheshire is the oldest of all the English cheeses and is referred to in the Domesday Book, although it is thought to date back to pre-Roman times. It is actually a scalded curd cheese, the curds being heated in the whey before being drained. Cheshire is actually sold when it is one to two months old, but it can be matured for over a year. Farmhouse cheeses are bandaged in cloth and either dipped in wax or larded. Blue Cheshire is hard to find but worth the search. It is sharp and strong, the blueing being achieved by the introduction of the Roquefort *penicillium*.

Double Gloucester is rich orange in colour and is made from the morning and evening milkings of Guernsey cattle. One or two farms make the cheese with milk from the Old Gloucester cattle, from which it was traditionally made, and the resulting cheese is quite delicious. The cheese is firm in texture and has a strong flavour. This cheese is often whipped when factory made and combined with other cheeses or flavourings, eg 'Cotswold' being Double Gloucester with herbs.

Lancashire is the perfect answer for people who do not like grating cheese - it crumbles very easily for adding to sauces and salads, etc. Factory made Lancashire cheese can be very mild, but the farmhouse varieties are wonderful. The curds of two days' cheesemaking are mixed together before being milled and pressed. Lancashire is the best cheese to use in place of the Greek Feta when you return from holiday but still hanker after the sun.

Leicester - usually called Red Leicester - melts quickly and evenly. With its strong colour it is an ideal cheese for cooking in a microwave as it will add colour to dishes that would not otherwise brown. Many people ask for farmhouse Leicester in my shop, in preference to the pre-packed factory-produced variety.

Sage Derby is the most common way to buy Derby cheese, which is a great pity as a mature, plain Derby is stronger than a one-year-old Cheddar, but very difficult to find. To produce the green veining in Sage Derby, the leaves of this very pungent herb are soaked in chlorophyll and the resulting juice, rather than the chopped leaves themselves, is added to the cheese. A very subtle flavour results.

THE NUTRITIVE VALUE OF CHEESE

Cheese is a protein of high biological value and a little goes a long way. Although primarily a protein food, cheese has a high fat content and care should be taken when eating it if you are following a strict diet for health or cosmetic reasons.

As a general rule, the softer cheeses are less fattening. This does not mean that they have a lower percentage fat content but that the fat present is partly mixed with the liquid that is retained in the cheese. Hard cheeses are more fatty, the whey having been pressed out of the cheese to leave only the fatty curds. The worst thing about dieting is giving up cheese.

Stilton is the king of English cheeses, but is as variable as English weather. If you like a mild cheese, buy pasteurised Stilton, but for the true flavour of the cheese, do look out for the unpasteurised cheeses. Prime Stilton is available from the autumn onwards, being made with summer milk. These cheeses have a slightly yellower paste than the Stiltons available at other times of the year and are perfect for eating at Christmas. Stilton is blued by using the Roquefort *penicillium* and should always be creamy and not crumbly. Left-over Stilton is very good for cooking and is an affordable substitute for Roquefort. White Stilton is a very young, immature Stilton and does not compare to the traditional blue variety, although I like it in salads and for cooking, where its slightly sharp flavour is penetrating.

Wensleydale is crumbly, being only lightly pressed, and is the traditional cheese of the North for eating with apple pies, fruit and cake. Like Cheshire, Wensleydale is an ancient cheese, made originally by the monks at Jervaulx Abbey. Many of its contemporaries, such as Coverdale and Swaledale, which never transferred to large-scale factory production, have recently been revived, but Wensleydale is the best known of this group.

These traditional cheeses have now been joined by a host of other British cheeses, some based on ancient recipes but others on new ideas, and British cheesemaking is enjoying a glittering renaissance. Farmhouse cheeses are being made throughout the British Isles and many are available all over the country through specialist cheese shops. It is, however, difficult for the cheesemaker to equate maintaining quality and making money. Cheesemaking is very labour-intensive and the producer must be dedicated to his art to maintain his enthusiasm.

The cheesemaker has the best control over his cheese if he is able to use the milk from his own flock or herd - he then knows exactly what he is getting and where the animals have been grazed as the type of grass and subsoil contributes much to the flavour of the milk and then the cheese. The following are some of my favourite farmhouse British cheeses that you should be able to get without too much difficulty:

(*l to r*) Burndell goats' milk cheese; Cheddar; Cheshire; Dunsyre Blue; Wheatland; Belstone; Swaledale; Castle Hill; Wheatland Moor (*at front*); Wellington; Teifi; Malthouse Coulommier goats' milk cheeses

Castle Hill is a Sussex Cheddar-type cheese made on a large scale but only from the milk of a single Friesian herd. As it is unpasteurised, it is strong and rounded.

Lanark Blue & Dunsyre Blue are made in Scotland from ewes' milk and cows' milk respectively. Lanark Blue is very similar to Roquefort and nearly as expensive, but the Dunsyre Blue is more affordable and has a creamy yet pungent flavour.

Llangloffan is my favourite of the harder Welsh cheeses. It can be sold mild when young, or matured to a greater depth of flavour. It is always creamy, being made from Jersey milk.

Milleens is an Irish soft cheese with a washed rind, similar to Port Salut. It is clean and fresh, although well flavoured.

Pencarreg is a soft Welsh organic Brie, made from unpasteurised milk, so has a full flavour.

Single Gloucester is another traditional cheese that is enjoying a revival. It should be made from just the morning milk taken from Old Gloucester cows. It is softer and milder than Double Gloucester and, although it tastes creamy, is relatively low in fat.

Spenwood is a delightful sheep's milk cheese from the same dairy as the Wellington. It is hard, like the Spanish sheep's milk cheese Manchego, and has a flavour that is slightly similar to Gruyère. It cooks well and is particularly useful for children who are allergic to cows' milk cheeses, although all sheep's milk cheeses are expensive for everyday use.

Swaledale is a traditional cheese of the same era as Wensleydale, which has been revived and is now selling well. It is slightly creamier than Wensleydale, but is also lightly pressed so it always has a soft texture. Swaledale is beautiful when first cut. If your cheesemonger cuts a Swaledale for the person in front of you, make sure that you take a piece as well.

Teifi is best described as Welsh Edam, being very similar in texture and flavour. It is sold with various flavourings added, such as garlic, chives, peppers, etc. Like Edam, Teifi is waxed and keeps well.

Wellington is made from Guernsey milk from the Duke of Wellington's cattle and processed in vats that were originally used for making Edam. The cheese is most similar to a good Double Gloucester and is very creamy in flavour. The cheeses are matured in cellars at Stratfield Saye, the country home of the Duke.

Wheatland & Wheatland Moor are made in Devon in the style of traditional French cheeses, the Wheatland being like the best farmhouse Brie and the Moor following a recipe for Port Salut. Both are made on a farm that uses only calcified seaweed to fertilise the ground.

There are many stories concerning man's first attempts at making cheese. Mammals were first domesticated for their milk around 6000BC and cheesemaking was a natural progression from the acid that formed naturally in the milk and curdled it. The most popular legend concerning true cheesemaking is that of a herdsman who put fresh milk into an animal's stomach pouch that had not been cleaned and sterilised and discovered that the action of the remaining rennet reacted with the milk to form a sweet cheese, as opposed to the known acid variety.

Cheeses have evolved throughout history and new varieties are still being made today. The early travellers who returned from all parts of the world with new recipes and ideas for incorporating herbs and spices did much to widen the knowledge of cheesemaking techniques.

All cheeses are made in basically the same way, by heating milk to separate the curds from the whey and then cutting the curds before pressing to yield the finished cheese. The type of milk used and additives to the natural ingredients will all affect the finished cheese, as will the actual process of making the cheese.

Factory-made cheeses are manufactured in huge quantities and each process is mechanised. The stirring is automatic, the cutting is done by machine and the milling is done by a machine working on the principle of a giant food processor. Such mechanisation produces very consistent results throughout the year, but the cheeses often lack the authentic flavour of handmade varieties.

CHEESEMAKING
Then & Now

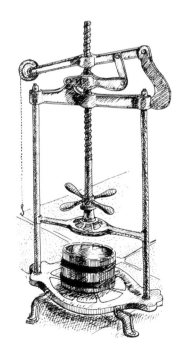

CHEESEMAKING NOW -
The Old-fashioned Way

The revival of small-scale farmhouse cheeses and the subsequent interest in these individual products has been brought about partly by the farmers' need to cut the amount of milk that they send to the Milk Marketing Board and partly by the public's demand for 'real' cheeses with traditional texture and flavour.

I was lucky enough to join the makers of Gospel Green, a Sussex-made hard cheese, to watch the cheesemaking in process. Here is a true marriage of traditional methods and equipment with modern health and hygiene requirements - their vat,

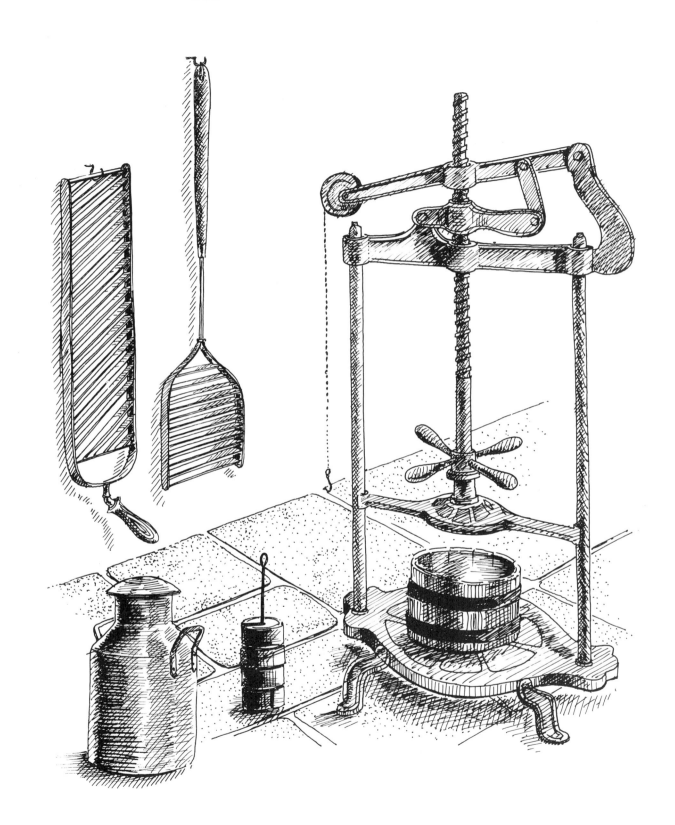

tools and press are old equipment that was purchased from an elderly cheesemaker some twenty years ago, together with the recipe for the cheese. I had a relatively easy morning, joining James and Cathy Lane once the 409 litres (90gal) of Friesian milk was in the vat in the dairy at 7.30am (they had risen at 5.30 to do the milking). One cow will yield up to 23 litres (5gal) of milk and 4½ litres (1gal) should make 450g (1lb) of cheese.

The Lanes' vat has had to be fitted with a new stainless steel liner. It is held in a double-skinned tank which is filled with hot water to raise the temperature of the milk. An enzyme starter culture is added to the milk at 1.1°C (30°F) and stirred for 5min with a curd fork. This starts to raise the acidity of the milk and thus to curdle it. Un-pasteurised milk, such as used for Gospel Green cheese, will curdle naturally through the action of the bacteria that is present when the milk is heated, but the addition of the starter culture, which must always be used when cheese is made from pasteurised milk, hastens the process. After a period of time, the milk appears to skin; this is the cream rising to the surface of the vat. Rennet is added to the vat, then the milk is deep stirred, right to the bottom of the tank, to ensure that the rennet is thoroughly mixed, and the top is stirred to keep the cream properly blended.

After a period of some 45min, the vat appeared full of blancmange. The curds could be pulled away from the edge of the vat, in the same way as a cooked Victoria sandwich can be lightly pulled away from the edge of a cake tin, and the curd could be cut in a straight line with a finger. The curds are then cut with a curd knife, from top to bottom and from side to side, and, after a short time, the curd sinks to the bottom of the vat and the whey rises.

The temperature in the vat is then raised very slowly to 3.3°C (38°F). This process must not be rushed or the final cheese will be of poor quality and liable to develop faults while it matures. The developing cheese must be stirred throughout this process. I visited the Lanes on a very cold day and the correct temperature was eventually obtained within the vat by flushing hot water through the double skin of the liner. The curds were left to settle to the bottom of the vat, a process known as pitching.

The whey, which is ideal for feeding to pigs, is then drained from the vat. Cheesemaking only becomes totally economic if all the products from the process can be used. The curds are lifted onto muslin-covered racks and cut through with a knife before they are left to drain. The cutting and draining is done twice. The curds are now quite hard and at this stage resemble a chunky cottage cheese crossed with the homemade cheese or paneer as used in Indian cookery.

The drained curd, now a solid mass, is turned out of the muslin and the really hard work of milling begins. The firm curd is squeezed through the cheesemaker's fingers to break it into small particles - they must be small or the finished cheese will be of an uneven texture. I imagine that this would be a good finger exercise for resting concert pianists - after the first few minutes my digits were dead! Salt is then lightly worked into the curds before they are packed into muslin-lined truckles or moulds. The Gospel Green wooden truckle ends have had to be replaced with pvc equivalents to satisfy current health standard requirements. The truckles are lightly pressed for 24hr, then turned and pressed more firmly for a further 24hr period, during which more whey is lost from the cheese.

After 48hr the cheeses are trimmed and wrapped in sterilised muslin, which is stuck to the cheese with a flour and water paste. The cheeses are matured in a specially constructed humid cellar for 2½-3 months, during which time they lose a further 225-325g/8-12oz in weight and develop a mould or rind beneath the muslin.

Cheesemaking by hand is a long and tiring process - it sounds idyllic but is very hard, physical work. Turning a full cellar of Gospel Green cheeses can take up to 2hr and each cheese must be turned every day. When I visited the dairy we left at 2pm, after cleaning the walls, floor and all the cheesemaking equipment. Handmade cheeses are justifiably more expensive than the factory-produced equivalents and are, in my opinion, worth every penny.

GOSPEL GREEN is a close-textured cheddar-type cheese with a full and distinctive flavour. It is available by post, except in the summer months when there may be a seasonal shortage. For further details contact James & Cathy Lane, Gospel Green Cottage, nr Haslemere, Surrey.

SHEEP'S & GOATS' MILK CHEESES

Any animal that can be milked can provide the raw material for making cheese. It is said that yaks' milk is sometimes used and in Italy buffalos' milk is made into cheese. However, cows' milk is the standard, but there is a growing market for cheeses made from the milk of sheep or goats. They tend to have a distinctive, pungent flavour and are quite different from other cheeses. The curds are often whiter and paler. Ewes' milk cheese is generally hard, while goats' milk varieties may be processed in many ways.

Of all the ewes' milk cheeses, Roquefort is surely the best known. Roqueforts exported from France are often well salted to improve their keeping qualities, but the variety produced in France has a well-balanced, almost delicate flavour. Production of Roquefort is strictly controlled and the cheeses are stamped in red with a picture of a sheep to show that they are genuine, made with milk from Larzac sheep and matured in caves in Combalou. Roquefort is always foil wrapped as this prevents a rind from forming on the cheese.

Pecorino, Feta and Manchego are the best known of the remaining ewes' milk cheeses. The first, from Italy, is a hard grana cheese and is excellent for all Italian cookery. It is sharper than Parmesan and combines well with pasta (see Pesto alla Genovese, p23). Pecorino Romano is the best variety of this cheese and has a white, waxy rind. Feta is a much softer ewes' milk cheese and is made throughout the eastern Mediterranean. It is delicious in salads of onion, tomato and juicy black olives, sprinkled with fresh oregano. Of all the Spanish cheeses, Manchego is the only one to be widely available outside Spain. The pure ewes' milk cheese is of a better flavour than the cheaper mixed milk version and it also has a very dry texture.

The French make countless varieties of goats' milk cheeses which are often small and wrapped in a chestnut leaf and then tied with raffia (see p67). Chèvre is the best known of all the goats' milk cheeses, possibly because the name is actually a generic term for all goats' milk cheese. It is usually sold in a log and displayed on straw.

English goat-keepers are now producing some excellent cheeses - I stock four that are all made in Sussex. Fresh goats' milk cheese is available in many supermarkets and has a slightly sharper flavour than fromage frais. Some goats' milk cheeses are lightly pressed and then rolled in herbs, while others are soft, unpressed, surface-ripened cheeses made in the Coulommiers style. I keep one pressed goats' milk cheese, Burndell, which has a creamy texture and a mild flavour. It is waxed like an Edam and is quite delicious. Many goats' milk cheeses are produced organically by small-scale farmers and smallholders.

Both ewes' and goats' milk cheeses are often sold in olive oil, flavoured with herbs and spices and they are delicious. Usually eaten cold with the flavoured oil spooned over, these cheeses are also excellent when placed under a very hot grill until browned.

96

BLUE CHEESES

There are many varieties of blue cheeses, most of which are produced by introducing a controlled *penicillium* into the paste during ripening, although a few cheeses do blue naturally. Most blue cheeses are cheeses in their own right, but others are treated versions of existing cheeses, eg Cheshire and Blue Cheshire. The *penicillium* is often introduced to the cheeses by syringe and spreads through the tiny gaps between the lightly pressed curds. Nearly all blue cheeses are scalded and lightly pressed and tend to crumble. It is virtually impossible to grate them, so they should be broken up by stroking with a fork if required for cooking. Like Roquefort (see p96), most blue cheeses are wrapped in foil to prevent any skin or crust from forming on the cheese. It is therefore unreasonable to question the fact that the cheese is weighed with the foil on if you normally buy a rinded cheese that is weighed with the outer crust.

The British blue cheeses are described on pp86-92. Of the French cheeses, Bleu d'Auvergne and Forme d'Ambert are my favourites, in addition to Roquefort. Both are creamy and slightly sharp with a close and even blueing. Many other varieties of French blue cheeses are available both in France and in cheese shops throughout the world. Danish Blue is one of the best known of the blue cheeses, but it is very sharp and unrefined. Blau Castello is a relatively new Danish cheese with a very creamy paste and slightly sharp but tempered flavour.

The Italians make wonderful blue cheeses of which the best known are Gorgonzola, from Lombardy, and Dolcelatte, which literally means sweet milk. The best Gorgonzolas should be clean and sharp and almost green in appearance rather than blue. Blue cheeses are used quite extensively in Italian cooking and Gorgonzola is much better for this purpose than the slightly sweeter Dolcelatte.

Of the remaining blue cheeses, Mycella is probably the best known. It is sometimes called Danish Gorgonzola, although the veining is greenish in colour and the paste is very yellow. Mycella is relatively mild for a blue cheese.

THE SPICE OF LIFE

Some foods would be very bland without the judicious use of spices and other seasonings. Many cuisines that are based on grains and pulses make extensive use of a wide range of spices to flavour their foods and this can clearly be seen in Indian and Far Eastern cookery.

◈

The following spices are shown on p99 and are some of the most popular

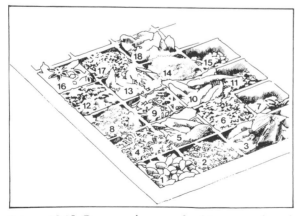

Spices: 1&15 Green cardamoms; 2 white mustard seed; 3 bay leaves; 4 cumin seeds; 5 cassia bark; 6 fenugreek seeds; 7&18 brown cardamoms; 8 turmeric; 9 cloves; 10 chillis; 11&12 peppercorns; 13 mace; 14 desiccated coconut; 16 star anise; 17 white poppy seeds

THE
SPICE
OF LIFE

Bay leaves Bay trees grow well in almost any country and the dried leaves are added to many stews and casseroles, as well as to countless other dishes. Bay leaves should always be broken to release their flavour which is mainly contained in the stalk. I think that bay is very underrated and should be used more by itself to reveal its flavour.

Black peppercorns are an essential spice for any form of cookery (see p57).

Cardamoms can be green or black and are a collection of aromatic seeds contained in a pod which must be split to release the full flavour. Cardamoms are used to flavour rice and, after saffron, are the world's most expensive spice.

Cassia bark is the Oriental version of cinnamon and can be used as a dried bark or ground into powder form.

Chillis are very hot, dried peppers. Do not rub your eyes when preparing them. They are native to South America and are used mainly in Mexican cookery, although some Indian recipes also include them.

Cloves are dried flower buds and are usually sold whole. Ground cloves, if available, can produce a delicious flavour in Christmas puddings. Cloves are very aromatic and can be used for their scent, as in orange pomanders, as well as for their ability to flavour both sweet and savoury dishes.

Cumin Seeds are used in curries and also extensively in Mexican cookery. The seeds are often ground and the resulting powder is a basic ingredient of curry spice mix.

Desiccated coconut is not strictly a spice but is a basic ingredient for many curries as well as being used extensively for cakes and desserts.

Fenugreek is often sold as dried seeds but is really more useful in powder form, when it is a vital ingredient in many curries.

Mace is the outer husk of the nutmeg and has a strong but fragrant flavour. I combine mace with bay, especially for seasoning pork or oily fish, such as herrings.

Star anise is a dried pod containing anise seeds. It is used in Chinese cookery.

Turmeric is the ground root of a member of the ginger family. It has little flavour and is used mainly to colour foods. If you cannot afford saffron use turmeric, but you will miss the delicate fragrance of the Spanish spice.

White mustard seeds These hot seeds are used for English mustard (see p60).

White poppy seeds are less common than blue, and are used mainly in Indian and Jewish cookery. They have a distinctive nutty flavour and texture.

Other spices that you may only be able to find in a delicatessen include juniper berries, which are used to flavour gin and are essential when cooking game casseroles; tamarind seed, which is really a dried pulp and is used in curries; and annatto which is a small seed used in Latin American cookery. The outer casing is removed from these seeds and used as a food dye; it is used extensively on washed rind cheeses.

Pepper sauces are made mainly in South America, where the most famous of all is Tabasco sauce. Tabasco is so well known that it is to pepper sauces what Hoover is to vacuum cleaners. It is named after the Tabasco region of Mexico where the peppers used in its production are grown. They are very hot - much stronger than any fresh chillis that are available in the UK. The peppers are pulped, then left to mature for three years before being distilled with vinegar. The seeds and skins of the peppers are removed from the sauce which is then bottled. Tabasco can be added to casseroles and rice dishes. I find it rather overpowering in fish recipes, but it is used extensively in Creole cookery and in dishes such as seafood gumbo. As a change from the very fiery nature of Tabasco, I sometimes enjoy the slightly sweeter, thicker, opaque chilli sauces from Indo-China. These have a roundness that belies their heat.

Sambals are also pepper sauces, although reduced to give a thick relish used as a chutney (see p54). These are used in Indonesian and Thai cookery.

FIESTA FOODS

(*l to r*) Beef & Chilli Stew; Guacamole;
Tortilla Chip Pie; Cebiche; Four Bean Salad

Mexican food is becoming more and more popular. Chilli con carne is an established favourite and many shops stock the ingredients for making tacos - crispy pancake envelopes that contain a deliciously spicy meat or fish filling, all topped with salad and a tangy tomato sauce.

Delicatessens often stock a wider range of Mexican ingredients to enable you to produce authentically flavoured dishes. These should include mild and hot peppers (the jalapeño pepper is not for the faint hearted), and tomato sauces for tacos which can also be used for many other dishes. It is often advisable to use the commercially prepared seasonings for tacos and chilli as many of the varieties of red and chilli peppers that are abundant in Mexico cannot be obtained easily in other countries.

I have chosen the following recipes to show the versatility of Mexican food. They are all relatively quick to prepare and could be combined for a Mexican buffet party. Simple salads of lettuce, tomatoes and olives may accompany most of the main dishes.

Avocado Soup
Serves 4

This vivid green soup is a colourful beginning to any meal. It is usually served well chilled, but may also be eaten warm. Do not boil the soup, especially if you add soured cream or natural yogurt.

750ml/1½pt/3¾ cups chicken stock
3 ripe avocados
1 can Mexican green chillis in brine (approx 125g/ 4oz), drained
salt and pepper
soured cream or natural yogurt (optional)

1 · Cool the chicken stock, then place in a blender or food processor with the flesh of the avocados, half the green chillis and a little salt and pepper. Process until smooth.
2 · Turn into a serving dish and chill in the refrigerator for 1-2hr.
3 · Chop the remaining chillis and serve them with the chilled soup, after adding 2-3×15ml/tbsp soured cream or natural yogurt, if required.

Mexican Tomato Soup
Serves 4

A spicy variation on a traditional favourite in any country. Tostada shells may be served with this soup; they are flat fried tortilla pancakes which require heating in a moderate oven for a few minutes before serving.

2×15ml/tbsp oil
1 large onion, chopped
1 clove garlic, crushed
1 green pepper, chopped
1×400g/14oz can chopped tomatoes
1 packet taco seasoning mix
500ml/1pt/2½ cups boiling chicken stock

1 · Heat the oil in a large saucepan, add the onion, garlic and green pepper and cook until soft.
2 · Add the chopped tomatoes, the taco seasoning mix and the stock. Cover and simmer for 20min.
3 · Season to taste if necessary, and serve with croûtons, tortilla chips or heated tostada shells.

Tortilla Chip Pie
Serves 4–6 (see p103)

This is a very good way of introducing the family to Mexican food. The pastry case contains a spicy beef taco filling and the grated cheese topping browns in the oven to give a tempting appearance.

1×22cm/8in pre-baked pastry case
450g/1lb minced beef
1 packet taco seasoning mix
150ml/6fl oz/¾ cup water
1 ripe avocado, peeled and sliced (optional)
4 tomatoes, sliced
50-75g/2-3oz Cheddar cheese, grated
tortilla chips to serve

1 · Pre-heat the oven to gas mark 5/190°C/ 375°F. Place the pastry case on a baking sheet.
2 · Cook the minced beef in a saucepan over a high heat until browned. Drain off any fat. Add the taco seasoning mix and the water, stir well and simmer for 20min.
3 · Pile the meat into the pastry case and top with the sliced tomatoes and then the grated cheese.

Place in the pre-heated oven for 30-40min, until the cheese is golden brown.

4 · Before serving, arrange the tortilla chips around the pie on top of the cheese.

COOK'S NOTE: *A layer of soured cream may be added to the pie for extra flavour. I find it best to spread the cream over the minced beef, and then to top that with the avocado (if used) and the tomato.*

Four Bean Salad
Serves 6 (see p103)

There are many variations on this popular and filling salad. Use the beans of your choice, but do include red kidney beans.

175g/6oz green beans
175g/6oz broad beans
1×400g/14oz can chick peas
1×400g/14oz can red kidney beans
100ml/4fl oz vinaigrette dressing
good pinch ground chilli
salt and pepper to taste

1 · Cook the green and broad beans in boiling salted water until just tender. Drain and refresh immediately by steeping them in cold water.

2 · Drain and rinse the chick peas and kidney beans and combine with the other beans.

3 · Add the chilli to the vinaigrette dressing, pour over the salad and toss. Chill well, then toss again before serving.

Guacamole
Serves 8 (see p102)

No Mexican party would be complete without this renowned avocado dip.

2 large avocados, peeled and stoned
juice of 1 lime
1 jar taco tomato sauce, mild or hot
2 cloves garlic, crushed
salt to taste
coriander sprigs or chilli powder to garnish
tortilla chips to serve

1 · Place the avocados, lime juice, taco sauce and garlic in a blender or food processor and process until smooth. Season to taste with salt and transfer to a serving bowl.

2 · Garnish the guacamole with chilli powder or coriander sprigs, then serve in the centre of a plate of tortilla chips.

Turkey with Mexican Mole Pepper Sauce
Serves 4

Turkey with Mexican Mole Pepper Sauce is based on a classic dish, eaten throughout Mexico, of turkey cooked in a fried chilli sauce - this is to Mexicans what curry is to Indians. The classic dish may require preparation over a period of two days, but this simple variation is much quicker. The big talking point is the addition of grated chocolate to darken and enrich the sauce. Don't worry about the mole - it's the Mexican word for sauce! This dish equates to a vindaloo curry and should be eaten with respect.

3×15ml/tbsp oil
1×200g/7oz can jalapēno peppers, drained and chopped
1×113g/4oz can Mexican green chillis in brine, drained and chopped
2 cloves garlic, crushed
4 large turkey breasts, skinned and beaten
50g/2oz toasted sesame seeds
450g/1lb tomatoes, chopped
125g/4oz salted roast peanuts
½×5ml/tsp ground aniseed
6 cloves
freshly ground black pepper
500ml/1pt/2½ cups boiling chicken stock
4×15ml/tbsp tomato purée
40g/1½oz bitter cooking chocolate
salt
plain boiled rice and salad to serve

1 · Heat the oil in a large flameproof casserole dish and cook the jalapēnos, chillis and garlic until softened. Add the turkey breasts and cook until browned on both sides.

2 · Add half the sesame seeds to the casserole with the tomatoes, peanuts, aniseed, cloves, pepper and stock. Bring to the boil, then cover and simmer very slowly for 1-1½hr, until the turkey is tender.

3 · Remove the turkey from the pan and keep warm on a serving dish.

4 · Liquidise the sauce. Add the tomato purée, grated chocolate and salt and pepper to taste.

5 · Heat the sauce gently until all the ingredients are well combined.

6 · Serve the turkey breasts sprinkled with the remaining sesame seeds and with the sauce handed separately.

Beef & Green Chilli Stew
Serves 6 (see p102)

This is a rich, satisfying casserole with more than a taste of the exotic, but which could be included in nearly any dinner party menu. The green chillis used are the milder of the Mexican peppers. Tostada shells may be served in place of potatoes.

3×15ml/tbsp oil
1 large onion, sliced (use a red onion if
 possible)
2 cloves garlic, crushed
675g/1½lb braising steak, trimmed and
 cubed
1 packet taco seasoning mix
1×400g/14oz can chopped tomatoes
1 can Mexican green chillis in brine, drained
 and chopped
1×400g/14oz can Mexican refried beans
salt and pepper
parsley to garnish

1 · Pre-heat the oven to gas mark 4/180°C/350°F.

2 · Heat the oil in a large pan, add the onion and garlic and cook until soft.

3 · Toss the beef in the taco seasoning mix, then add to the pan and brown the meat on all sides.

4 · Add the chopped tomatoes, chillis and refried beans to the casserole with a little salt and pepper.

5 · Bring to the boil, then cover and cook in the pre-heated oven for 2hr or until the beef is tender.

6 · Season to taste and sprinkle with parsley before serving.

Nachos
Serves 12

This is the basic recipe for nachos - Mexican canapés. You may add other toppings if you wish, but always use refried beans as the base. Nachips are small round tortilla pancakes. A slice of chorizo sausage may be placed on top of the refried beans for variety. Chorizo is used widely in Mexican food, showing the strong Spanish influence.

1 packet nachips
1×400g/14 oz can refried beans
125g/4oz Cheddar cheese, grated
1 can Mexican green chillis in brine, drained
 and chopped
 or 1 can jalapeño peppers, drained and sliced
 or black olives for garnish

1 · Spread the nachips with a thickish layer of refried beans and place them in a grill pan on a rack.

2 · Scatter a little grated cheese over the nachos and top each one with either chopped green chillis, jalapeno slices or olives.

3 · Place under a hot grill until the cheese has melted. Serve immediately.

Cebiche
Serves 4 (see p103)

Like the Japanese, the Mexicans eat raw fish. In this variation on a very traditional recipe, the fish is marinaded in lime juice and takes on a white, cooked appearance. Serve as a starter or a lunch or supper dish.

450g/1lb fresh white fish fillets, eg cod, haddock,
 plaice, etc
juice of 6 limes, or 4 limes and 2 lemons
1 jar mild taco tomato sauce
salt and pepper
½×5ml/tsp dried oregano
2×15ml/tbsp olive oil
rice salad or warmed pitta bread for serving

1 · Skin the fish, remove any bones and cut into bite-sized pieces. Place the fish in a small china dish and add the lime juice, making sure that all the fish is completely covered.

2 · Cover the dish and place in the refrigerator for at least 5hr, until the fish has turned white and has a cooked appearance. Stir the fish carefully once or twice during marinading.

3 · Carefully stir the taco sauce, salt and pepper, oregano and olive oil into the fish. Chill for a further 45-60min.

4 · Serve with rice salad or warmed pitta bread.

Fish Tales

Quails' Eggs with Gravadlax

Delicatessens stock an interesting selection of canned fish and they will always stock smoked salmon. The best smoked salmon is definitely Scotch; it has a pinker appearance than the inferior Canadian salmon. Pre-sliced salmon should never be chunky or fatty and should be evenly sliced. Trimmings are a good buy for making into pâtés and dips. I have also made a very rich soup from smoked salmon pieces, but be very cautious about your fish stock if it is not to be spoiled by excessive salt. I think that smoked salmon in quiches in rather an extravagance.

Gravadlax makes a delicious alternative to smoked salmon and is the raw fish marinated with plenty of herbs, especially dill. It may be used in salads, as on p107, or served with a mustard-based sauce and brown bread and butter as a starter. Gravadlax can be more expensive than the best smoked salmon.

The best canned fish is further improved if it is steeped in olive oil rather than a cheaper vegetable oil. Sardines and anchovies are worth extra money if canned in olive oil and their flavour is greatly improved, even if you do not eat the oil. Gaffelbitter are tiny Scandinavian herring fillets and can be purchased in a variety of sauces, of which red wine and sherry are the most popular. They are traditionally served to accompany egg dishes. Use them in egg mayonnaise, omelettes or simply to top scrambled eggs.

Of the various smoked shellfish available, smoked mussels and oysters are the most popular, and smoked squid is the sort of thing that browsers pick up, show to their friends and put down again. Mussels and oysters are usually canned in cotton seed oil which is very strong, so they should be well rinsed before use and, if necessary, tossed in a little olive oil to restore their flavour. They are best used for cocktail savouries, but the cheaper mussels make a very tasty pasta sauce.

SMOKING IS GOOD FOR YOU!

Smoking is a very ancient art that has been used for hundreds of years to preserve fish and meat, preferred to salting because it does not destroy the natural flavour of the food to the same extent. Gutted raw fish are smoked slowly over wood chips and it is generally agreed that oak gives the best flavour, although other woods are preferred in some part of the world. Smoking takes place in a smokehouse which is linked by a pipe to a firebox. The smoke is directed across the food and out of the smokehouse. It is a very gentle process and the length of time required to complete the smoking depends on the size of the fish or meat to be processed.

Home smokeries may be purchased or made in large tins or drums.

Quails' Eggs with Gravadlax
Serves 4

125g/4oz gravadlax, finely sliced and chopped
125g/4oz chunk cucumber, finely diced
240g/approx 8oz tub natural Greek yogurt
salt and freshly ground black pepper
12 quails' eggs
green or blue food colouring
salad garnish

1 · Combine the gravadlax, cucumber and yogurt in a bowl, add salt and white pepper to taste. Leave in the refrigerator for the flavours to blend for at least 1hr.
2 · Place the quails' eggs in a pan of boiling water

and boil for 3min. Drain and refresh immediately in cold water, cracking the egg shells to allow the eggs to cool more quickly.
3 · Lightly crush the shells of the eggs, then drop them into a very strong solution of water and food colouring (approx 40ml/1½fl oz to 125ml/5fl oz water). Leave the eggs to colour for 2-3hr. Carefully peel the eggs, then leave to dry.
4 · Make a small bed of salad on each plate, then top with the gravadlax and cucumber salad. Arrange three eggs on each plate and garnish with fresh dill or mint. Serve with warm fingers of pitta bread or Melba toast.

DRIED MUSHROOMS

One of the more unusual foods to be found in a delicatessen are dried mushrooms. These are grown mainly in France, although Italy and Poland also produce some varieties. The most common are ceps and chanterelles. The flavour of these mushrooms is superb and, although they are expensive, they are worth treating yourself to for a special occasion. Dried mushrooms keep for at least a year and 75g/3oz is equivalent to 450g/1lb of fresh ones. Wherever possible, keep the water that the mushrooms are soaked in for use in the recipe.

POT ROASTED BEEF WITH MUSHROOM & CREAM SAUCE
Serves 6-8

25g/1oz dried mushrooms, preferably ceps
500ml/1pt/2½ cups boiling water
25g/1oz butter
2 × 15ml/tbsp olive oil
1,800g/4lb joint boned and rolled rib of beef
1 clove garlic, crushed
few drops Tabasco sauce
salt and freshly ground black pepper
125ml/5fl oz/⅔ cup double or thick cream
1 egg yolk

1 · Place the mushrooms in a bowl and cover with the boiling water then leave to soak for at least 20min.
2 · Heat together the butter and olive oil in a large pan or casserole dish, until the butter has melted. Add the beef and cook quickly on all sides until browned. Remove the meat from the pan.
3 · Drain the mushrooms with a slotted spoon and add them to the fat and juices in the pan. Cover and sweat over a low heat for 4-5min, stirring once. Return the meat to the pan and add the juice from the mushrooms with the garlic and Tabasco sauce. Cook, tightly covered with a lid, for 2½hr,

until tender when tested with a fork.
4 · Remove the meat from the pan and allow to stand for a few minutes before slicing.
5 · Beat together the cream and egg yolk, then add to the pan. Cook slowly, stirring constantly, until thickened but do not allow the sauce to boil or the cream will curdle and the egg will scramble.

Season to taste, then serve over the sliced beef.

MUSHROOM SOUFFLÉS
Makes 36

These tiny soufflés make a delicious pre-dinner nibble and are strongly flavoured by the dried mushrooms.

36 pre-cooked pastry cocktail cases
25g/1oz dried mushrooms
25g/1oz butter
1 clove garlic, crushed
pinch mace
25g/1oz flour
125ml/5fl oz/⅔ cup soured cream
2 eggs, separated

1 · Place the mushrooms in a bowl and cover with boiling water. Leave for 15-20min, then drain and chop.
2 · Pre-heat the oven to gas mark 5/190°C/375°F. Place the pastry cases on baking sheets.
3 · Melt the butter in a pan, add the chopped mushrooms, garlic and mace and cook for 2-3min, until the mushrooms are soft. Add the flour and cook for a few seconds, then remove the pan from the heat and add the soured cream and the egg yolks. Beat well.
4 · Whisk the egg whites until stiff, then fold them into the mixture. Use to fill the pastry cases and bake immediately in the pre-heated oven for 10-12min, until set.
5 · Serve immediately.

These expensive, shrivelled and unappealing tomatoes possess an incredible flavour that is quite outstanding. Recently introduced to the UK, I hope that sun-dried tomatoes will remain essential for the kitchen store-cupboard for as long as olive oil, salt and pepper are there. Keep the opened jar in the refrigerator; the tomatoes are packed in olive oil which may become cloudy, but this will not affect the flavour.

Slightly cheaper sun-dried tomatoes are now available in dry form. Chop and add to casseroles or steep in boiling water for a few minutes before adding to salads.

Summer Lamb Ragout
Serves 6 (opposite)

This casserole uses summer vegetables with the addition of sun-dried tomatoes to give a wonderfully rich flavour. Passata and stock are used in preference to wine for the casserole, to allow the flavour of the young lamb and vegetables to dominate the dish.

2kg/4-4½lb shoulder of lamb
1×15ml/tbsp olive oil
15g/½oz butter
1 large onion, sliced
1 red pepper, seeded and sliced
1 green pepper, seeded and sliced
450g/1lb courgettes, trimmed and thickly sliced
2-3×15ml/tbsp freshly chopped rosemary and
  oregano, mixed
salt and pepper
900g/2lb fresh tomatoes, skinned, seeded and chopped
  plus
  2×15ml/tbsp tomato paste
  or 500ml/1pt/2½ cups passata
6 sun-dried tomato halves, chopped
freshly chopped parsley, to garnish

1 · Trim the shoulder of lamb of most of the fat, then remove the meat from the bone and cut into small pieces. Pre-heat the oven to gas mark 3/ 160°C/325°F.
2 · Heat the oil and butter together in a heavy pan or casserole dish, add the onion and peppers and cook until soft. Add the courgettes, cover, and cook slowly for 4-5min until all the vegetables are soft. Remove to a plate using a slotted spoon.
3 · Add the lamb to the pan and cook quickly on all sides until browned. Return the vegetables to the casserole dish, or turn the meat and vegetables from the pan into a casserole suitable for the oven.
4 · Add the herbs, some salt and pepper and the chopped tomatoes or passata to the casserole with the chopped sun-dried tomatoes.
5 · Place the casserole into the pre-heated oven and cook for 1½-2hr, until the lamb is tender.
6 · Season the casserole to taste with salt and pepper and garnish with freshly chopped parsley before serving.

Tomato, Lime & Basil Soup
Serves 4 (opposite)

This soup is sharp and fresh - delicious.

2×15ml/tbsp olive oil
1 onion, sliced
1 small clove garlic, crushed
900g/2lb tomatoes, roughly chopped
2 limes, grated rind and juice
1×15ml/tbsp freshly chopped basil
  or 1×5ml/tsp dried basil
250ml/10fl oz/1¼ cups vegetable stock
1 bay leaf
salt and pepper
8 halves sun-dried tomatoes
cream to serve

1 · Heat the oil in a large saucepan, add the onion and garlic, cover and cook over a moderate heat until the vegetables are soft, in about 3-4min.
2 · Add all the remaining ingredients. Bring to the boil, then cover and simmer for 25-30min. Cool slightly, then blend until smooth in a liquidiser or processor.
3 · Season the soup to taste, then reheat, if necessary.
4 · Swirl a little cream into the soup just before serving.

(front to back) Summer Lamb Ragout; Pizza; Tomato, Lime & Basil Soup

111

NIBBLES
& Fancy Bits

The eternal enigma for the cocktail party host or hostess is what to give the guests that is different and can preferably be eaten in one bite. I find that traditional cocktail foods are always very popular and Devils or Angels on Horseback are a guaranteed success. Dips should be fairly thick so that they do not drop off accompanying crudités, and fillings for pastry parcels and buns should be firm if the food is likely to be bitten and not eaten in one mouthful. I usually allow about eight mouthfuls per person for catering. Do not underestimate the time required to prepare a cocktail party - a four-course dinner often takes less time!

Devils on Horseback
Makes approx 30 (see p115)

A classic dish that benefits from using the very best prunes (pruneaux d'Agen, see p61) and bacon.

30 thin rashers back bacon
450g/1lb ready-to-eat prunes, pitted
wooden cocktail sticks
30 small croûtons, lightly fried

1 · Pre-heat the oven to gas mark 5/190°C/375°F.
2 · Stretch the bacon rashers using the back of a knife. Roll one rasher around each prune and secure with a cocktail stick.
3 · Place one devil on each croûton, pressing the cocktail stick into the bread and place on a baking sheet.
4 · Place in the pre-heated oven for approx 10min, until the bacon is cooked and lightly browned.
5 · Serve immediately. I usually leave the cocktail sticks to make it easier for people to pick the devils up when they are hot.

COOK'S NOTE: *Angels on Horseback are prepared in the same way, using oysters in place of prunes; canned oysters are very good for this purpose. I do find, however, that prunes are generally more popular.*

Taramasalata
Makes approx 225g/8oz (see p114)

This is now as internationally popular as holidays on the Greek islands, from whence the recipe hails. A traditional dish of the eastern Mediterranean, there are many different recipes for taramasalata. Tarama is the salted and dried roe of the grey mullet, but is more usual to use smoked cods' roe which is easily available from fishmongers and delicatessens. Commercial taramasalata is often spoiled by the addition of too much bread or too much oil.

2 slices of white bread, crusts removed
125g/4oz smoked cods' roe, skinned
juice of one large lemon
75-125ml/4-5fl oz/²/₃ cup olive oil
1 × 15ml/tbsp grated onion, squeezed dry
salt and pepper if required

1 · Soak the bread in water for about 10min - this will make it easier to combine with the roe. Squeeze dry.

2 · Place the roe, lemon juice and squeezed bread in a food processor or blender. With the motor running, slowly add the oil until the mixture is the consistency of a thick mayonnaise.

3 · Stir in the onion, add the salt and pepper or a little more lemon juice if required. Serve with crudités or fingers of pitta bread.

COOK'S NOTE: *I tend not to use virgin olive oil for this dip as I find the flavour too strong for the roe.*

Savoury Petits Choux
Makes approx 50 (see p115)

Tiny puffs of choux pastry may contain a variety of fillings. They always look attractive and make a very welcome change from vol-au-vents at a party. The pastry is easy to make.

75g/3oz butter
200ml/8fl oz/1 cup water
12× level 15ml/tbsp flour, sieved
3 eggs, beaten
beaten egg to glaze

1 · Pre-heat the oven to gas mark 7/225°C/425°F. Lightly grease two baking sheets.

2 · Place the butter and water in a saucepan and heat until the butter is melted. Bring to the boil, then shoot in the sieved flour. Quickly remove the pan from the heat while beating the mixture vigorously, until it leaves the sides of the pan and forms a ball. Cool slightly.

3 · Gradually add the egg, beating well after each inclusion, until the mixture is shiny and of piping consistency.

4 · Pipe tiny balls of pastry onto the prepared baking sheets, or not more than $1/2 × 5ml/tsp$ mounds if you do not have a piping bag.

5 · Brush each bun with a little beaten egg, then place in the pre-heated oven. Bake for 15min, then reduce the heat to gas mark 5/190°C/375°F and cook for a further 10min, or until the pastry is browned and crisp.

6 · Slit each bun with a sharp knife and place on a cooling rack until cold.

Suggested fillings
As these buns are so small, it is very important that the filling chosen should be smooth enough to pass through a fine pipe into the pastry. Flavoured cream cheese fillings are generally best. Pipe the filling into the buns and decorate the tops with any that is over. Sprinkle the filled buns with chopped herbs or lumpfish caviar as appropriate.

Cream cheese and Herbs (see p115). Beat 175g/6oz cream cheese until smooth, add 1-2×15ml/tbsp single cream or strained natural yogurt and 2× 15ml/tbsp freshly chopped herbs of your choice. Add salt and pepper to taste.

Curried cheese Add 1-2 × 5ml/tsp curry paste to 175g/6oz softened cream cheese. A little finely chopped fresh coriander may also be added for colour.

Cream cheese with anchovies Add a few drops of anchovy essence to 175g/6oz softened cream cheese, until the required flavour is reached. Add 1-2 × 15ml/tbsp single cream or strained yogurt, if necessary, to give a piping consistency.

COOK'S NOTE: *The petits choux may be served warm or cold. Do not overheat them or the filling will become soft: 5-8min in a moderate oven at gas mark 4/180°C/350°F should be sufficient.*

Tartlets in a Hurry
(see p114)

For those of you who invite people round for drinks on the spur of the moment, it is a very good idea to visit your local 'deli' and purchase a few packets of ready cooked canapé cups and miniature tartlet cases. These have a long shelf life and can be served hot or cold, making them a very good stand-by to have in the cupboard.

Suggested fillings
Fish or meat pâtés are a useful standby for fillings. Taramasalata may also be used, and any of the cream cheese fillings suggested above for Savoury Petits Choux. Garnish the tartlets with lumpfish roe, slices of olives or capers. If you have time, pipe a little flavoured butter around the tartlets to give them a professional finish.

(l to r) Taramasalata; Pâté Tartlets; Ginger & Coriander Rolls; Savoury Petits Choux; Devils on Horseback

Cheese & Pineapple Dip
Serves approx 30-40

If you are laying your cocktail party nibbles out on a table that the guests will see, it is a very good idea to have a centre-piece, to give a focal point to the display and some height as most nibbles are small and therefore low.

This dip is served in two scooped-out halves of a pineapple. Cut carefully through the leaves at the top of the pineapple so that some remain attached to each half of the fruit. Incidentally, the pineapple is a sign of hospitality, making this a very appropriate dish to serve at a party.

1 large pineapple, carefully cut in half lengthways
225g/8oz cream cheese
675g/1½lb cottage cheese
3×15ml/tbsp freshly chopped chives
325g/12oz Shropshire blue cheese, crumbled
salt and pepper
paprika to garnish
crudités to serve

1 · Scoop out the flesh of the pineapple halves, taking great care not to cut through the skin. Turn the shells upside down on kitchen paper to drain any juice while preparing the dip.
2 · Purée the pineapple flesh in a liquidiser or food processor.
3 · Beat the cream cheese until smooth. Sieve the cottage cheese and add it to the cream cheese and beat well. Gradually mix in the pineapple purée with the chives.
4 · Add the crumbled Shropshire blue cheese to the dip, then season to taste with salt and pepper.
5 · Spoon the dip into the pineapple shells and arrange them top to toe on a large serving plate.

Sprinkle lightly with paprika and serve with the crudités surrounding the fruits.

COOK'S NOTE: *Do not serve the dip too cold otherwise the flavours will be lost. If preparing this in advance of the party, leave the dip in a bowl in the refrigerator. Remove about an hour before the guests are expected and fill the pineapple shells, then leave to come up to room temperature.*

Ginger & Coriander Rolls
Makes approx 60 pinwheels (see p114)

This recipe was given to me by a well-travelled customer on her return from the USA. It will grace any cocktail party where the guests are adventurous.

225g/8oz crystallised ginger
4-6×15ml/tbsp fresh coriander leaves
10 thin slices bread, crusts removed
mayonnaise for spreading

1 · Chop the ginger very finely. Chop the coriander leaves and mix with the ginger. Alternatively, chop the ginger and coriander together in a food processor - this will produce a vibrant, bright green filling.
2 · Flatten the bread with a rolling-pin, then spread each slice thinly with mayonnaise.
3 · Spread the bread with the ginger and roll each slice up into a roll. Wrap tightly in cling film and refrigerate for 3-4hr or overnight.
4 · Cut the rolls into slices approx 1cm/½in thick. Arrange on a serving plate, cover and refrigerate until ready to serve.

GLOSSARY/INDEX

cheesemaker's own herd. A wide variety of these individual cheeses is now available
Four Bean Salad   p105
Fromage Frais & Cranberry Salad Dressing   p28

Garlic & Walnut Sauce for pasta   p84
Garlic Vinaigrette   p28
Ginger & Coriander Rolls   p116
Gravadlax   p108/*Raw salmon marinated with plenty of dill and often served with mustard sauce*
Guacamole   p105

Haggis   p15/*The famed dish of Scotland, made from sheep's intestines and served on many traditional feast days.*
Ham   pp16–21/*A whole leg of pork, cut from the carcase before curing*
Ham, Bayonne   p17/*A lightly smoked ham from south-west France*
Ham, Parma   pp16–17/*An Italian air-dried ham, served very thinly sliced*
Ham, Smithfield   p21/*Traditionally made from pigs fed on nuts, mainly acorns*
Ham, Virginia   p21/*Traditionally made from pigs fed on peaches and peanuts*
Ham, Westphalian   p17/*A German smoked ham*
Ham, York   p21/*A dry cured ham, traditionally eaten at Christmas*
Ham, Bradenham   p21/*English hams, cured in a mixture of juniper and molasses to give a very black appearance to the uncooked hams*
Haslet   p14/*An English spiced meat loaf made from pork and sold sliced*
Hoisin   p52/*Chinese barbecue, sweet and sour sauce*

Kidney Bean Tartlets   p41
Kidneys with Dijon Mustard Sauce   p76

Lamb & Caper Pies   p48
Lamb Ragout, Summer   p111
Lemon & Pistachio Pudding   p25

Marinated Green Olives   p44

Mettwurst   p14/*A smoked German spreading sausage*
Mexican foods   pp102–6
Mexican Tomato Soup   p104
Mie Noodles   p52/*Flat egg noodles, similar to egg pasta, used in Eastern cookery*
Mortadella   p14/*An Italian slicing sausage often flavoured with pistachio nuts*
Mushroom Soufflés   p109
Mustard   p60/*A spicy condiment made from ground mustard seeds and available in various strengths*

Nachos   p106
Nibbles & Fancy Bits   p112/*Cocktail party food*

Oils, cold pressed   p29/*Unrefined oils, extracted without heat, having a full flavour and natural colour. Also called virgin or extra virgin, according to acidity*
Oils, olive, grapeseed, sesame etc   p29/*Culinary oils with characteristic flavours for various culinary uses*
Olives   p42/*The fruits of the olive tree, eaten when ripe or crushed to make olive oil*
Olives, Marinated Green   p44
Organic Foods   p85/*Foods produced without the use of chemical at any stage, either to fertilise the land or to treat the crops or the food*
Oriental Beef   p54
Osso Bucco   p58

Panettone   p63
Pasta Sauces   pp82–4
Pasta, types of   p81/*Made from a stiff dough of flour and water or egg, rolled into many shapes before drying. Fresh pasta is also available. Cook and serve with a sauce*
Pastrami   p21/*Brisket of beef, salted and spiced then coated in peppercorns. Served very thinly sliced*
Pepper   p50/*A common seasoning obtained from the dried berries of the pepper plant. Usually ground into a powder before use.*
Pepper Sauces   p101/*Hot condiments made from a variety of chilli peppers and often matured for several*